TIM CROUCH: PLAYS ONE

Tim Crouch

PLAYS ONE

My Arm

An Oak Tree

ENGLAND

The Author

methuen | drama

LONDON • NEW YORK • OXFORD • NEW DELHI • SYDNEY

METHUEN DRAMA
Bloomsbury Publishing Plc
50 Bedford Square, London, WC1B 3DP, UK
1385 Broadway, New York, NY 10018, USA
29 Earlsfort Terrace, Dublin 2, Ireland

BLOOMSBURY, METHUEN DRAMA and the Methuen Drama logo
are trademarks of Bloomsbury Publishing Plc

First published in Great Britain by Oberon Books 2011
Reprinted 2015, 2019
This edition published by Methuen Drama 2022

A catalogue record for this book is available from the British Library.

A catalog record for this book is available from the Library of Congress.

ISBN: PB: 978-1-3503-2202-8
eBook: 978-1-8494-3519-2

Series: Modern Plays

To find out more about our authors and books visit www.bloomsbury.com
and sign up for our newsletters.

To my friends Karl James and Andy Smith

'...a new adventure in a new idiom...calls for spectators who are active interpreters, who render their own translation, who appropriate the story for themselves, and who ultimately make their own story out of it. An emancipated community is in fact a community of storytellers and translators.'

Jacques Rancière, *The Emancipated Spectator*

Contents

My Arm – Hayward Gallery, February 2003
© *Chris Dorley-Brown*

THANKS

All the people, theatres and galleries who have supported my work. All the second actors who have performed (and will perform) in *An Oak Tree*. Karl James and Andy Smith. Lisa Wolfe for producing me. Giles Smart and Nicki Stoddart at United Agents. Ruth Little, Mark Subias, John Retallack, Caryl Churchill, Peggy Paterson, Hettie Macdonald, Alastair Creamer, Thomas Kraus, Dan Jones, Hannah Reade, Hannah Ringham, Chris Goode, Adrian Howells, Esther Smith, Vic Llewellyn, Ben Ringham, Max Ringham, Alex Critoph, Pete Gill, Simon Crane, Chris Dorley-Brown, Jane Prophet and Michael Craig-Martin. Dinah Wood at Faber and Faber. Katherine Mendelsohn, Philip Howard, Dominic Hill and all at the Traverse Theatre. James Hogan, Charles Glanville, Andrew Walby, Sophie O'Reirdan, Melina Theocharidou and all at Oberon Books. Fiona Bradley and The Fruitmarket Gallery. Purni Morell and the National Theatre Studio. Dominic Cooke, Diane Borger, Kate Horton, and all at the Royal Court Theatre. Francisco Frazoa and Culturgest, Lisbon. Alan Rivett and Neil Darlison at Warwick Arts Centre. Kelly Kirkpatrick and Michael Ritchie at Center Theatre Group. Martin Platt and David Elliot at Perry Street Theatre in Exile. Stephen Bottoms and the Workshop Theatre, University of Leeds.

Julia Crouch. Nel, Owen & Joe. Pam and Colin.

Introduction

Back in 1996, as a young critic shortly to publish his first book – *The Theatre of Sam Shepard* – the opportunity arose for me to meet John Lion, the founding artistic director of San Francisco's Magic Theatre. This was the venue where Shepard had premiered several of his most celebrated plays, so Lion was a key figure in the story. Not only that, he had read my manuscript, declared himself very impressed with it, and was promising a bang-up jacket blurb to help sell it (which he later delivered). I was excited to meet him, but fifteen years later I can recall little about our conversation other than the moment when he looked sternly at me and declared: 'You really need to put your dick on the table and say that Sam is the most important American playwright since Eugene O'Neill.' I nodded politely, and silently disagreed, but the phrase stuck in my head. Had something been lost in translation between Lion's assertive, American masculinity and my awkwardly self-deprecating Englishness? Presumably, he imagined me thumping some huge lump of intellectual sausage onto his figurative table. Yet I, as an unknown twenty-something, couldn't help feeling that it would be more a case of small, pink chipolata.

Now, in my forties, and with a little bit more weight in the world, I am more than happy to – well – stick my neck out, and assert that the four Tim Crouch plays contained in this volume make up one of the most important bodies of English-language playwriting to have emerged so far in the twenty-first century. Of course, we're less than a dozen years into it, so the statement is still a little on the cautious side, but I can think of no other contemporary playwright who has asked such a compelling set of questions about theatrical form, narrative content, and spectatorial engagement. These texts provide the outlines for an extraordinary series of live events, in which Crouch himself always performs, and which he has honed and developed in collaboration with his two, ever-present directors, Karl James and

Andy Smith (a smith).[1] The published scripts cannot substitute for these theatrical experiences, as even a cursory reading of their opening stage directions should make clear: too much else is set in motion during performances of these plays for them to be adequately circumscribed by language. Nevertheless, the deft use *of* language – in a perfectly phrased line, or a cunningly placed speech – is one of the most vital, and under-appreciated, weapons in Crouch's dramatic armoury. These are plays that reward careful textual analysis, and their publication together will, I believe, help make that fact more widely appreciated.

It strikes me now that Lion's 'dick on the table' metaphor might help us begin to unpack some key features of Crouch's writing. Firstly, there is the sheer unexpectedness of the image. Had I been advised to 'stick my neck out' (an overly familiar, and thus 'dead' metaphor), I would probably have long since forgotten the whole exchange. Yet with a few simple words, Lion placed an image in my head that I haven't been able to shake since (much as I might have wanted to). Part of that has to do with the incongruous juxtaposition of everyday elements (dick, table), part of it with the information that Lion had *not* provided (what size of dick, what kind of table), and part of it with the unspoken but disturbing possibility of other items in the scenic vicinity (a kitchen knife? a rolling pin?). My imagination was activated – *made active* – by the choice of phrase, and indeed I probably ran with it much further than Lion intended. By setting the scene up but not 'filling it in', he made *me* its imaginative author. Tim Crouch, I would suggest, does something similar (though much more deliberate) by combining provocative spoken language with only a bare minimum of stage visuals: typically his plays are without sets, costumes or lighting plots. Instead, he strips the theatrical event down to the fundamental encounter between actors and audience – using a bare stage or, in the case of *The Author,* making the audience seating itself into the 'stage'. Our

1 Smith writes revealingly about this collaborative process in his article 'Gentle Acts of Removal, Replacement and Reduction: Considering the Audience in Co-Directing the Work of Tim Crouch.' *Contemporary Theatre Review*, Vol. 21 No. 4 (2011), pp. 410-415.

constant awareness, as spectators, of these raw theatrical facts is then put into play with what we are invited to see – in the 'mind's eye' – through the spoken word. For example, in his first play, *My Arm,* Crouch appears as performer-narrator to tell us a first-person narrative about a man who, as a boy, decided to hold his arm above his head and never take it down. Yet the performer himself never raises his arm above his head – so that a nagging question arises over the relationship between what is described and what is seen. Meanwhile, as stand-ins for the various other characters in the story, Crouch uses a random selection of small objects, borrowed from his audience and blown-up on a video screen: a set of keys stands in as the boy's mother, perhaps, or a lipstick as his brother. The lack of physical resemblance between the presented objects and the things they are made to represent creates a sense of humorous incongruity, but also allows the audience to bring in personal emotional associations of their own. I recall, in one performance, being strangely moved at seeing a pencil case and a can of body-spray bullying the Action Man doll which always stands in as the young 'Tim'. Precisely by *not* showing us what the bullies 'really' looked like, or having actors 'emote' their aggression, Crouch allowed me to fill in my own responsive associations with the scene described.

By Crouch's own account, *My Arm* was in part written as an emotional reaction of his own – to the state of most contemporary theatre as he experienced it. He had spent years as a jobbing actor, having to manufacture the appearance of emotions and having others pretending back at him. Plays were rehearsed into fixed patterns that seemed to Crouch to rob performances of any real 'liveness' or spontaneity, and indeed to rob spectators of any personal agency in the proceedings.[2] Everything was being *done* for them. Crouch set out to create a theatrical situation in which spectators had to do something for themselves, using their own imaginations and emotional resources. One might object, of course, that 'seeing with the mind's eye' is what one does when

2 Crouch discusses these concerns in his interview with Seda Ilter, "'A Process of Transformation": Tim Crouch on *My Arm.' Contemporary Theatre Review,* Vol. 21 No. 4 (2011), pp. 394-404.

reading a novel: we take the words on the page and extrapolate an imaginative world for ourselves. So, conversely, shouldn't theatre be about *showing* us something, from the stage? Well, yes it should – but of course, theatre can never show us everything. Unlike film, a medium in which any location or scale of events can be immediately presented to us visually (the earth from space; a watch on a table in a cafe in Algiers), theatre uses people and objects that are physically present as a means of invoking other people, places and ideas that are not. This interplay of the present and absent (which pertains to contemporary performance as much as traditional drama) means that theatre, almost by definition, involves a degree of collaborative involvement on the part of the audience: 'piece out our imperfections with your thoughts', suggests the Prologue to Shakespeare's *Henry V.*

Again, skeptics might counter that theatre must simply be an imperfect and limited medium – some kind of awkward half-way house between the pure imaginative space of the novel and the pure visual space of the cinema. At times, certainly, it can seem that way. Yet Crouch's work represents a compelling illustration of Dan Rebellato's argument that theatre's distinctive qualities as a medium reside in its being inherently *metaphorical* – that it works less by visual resemblance than by inviting us to see one set of things (be it actors and sets or keyrings and body-sprays) in terms of another. 'The first thing to note,' Rebellato observes,

> is that metaphor does not prescribe in advance what sort of connection must be made between the two objects it compares. Metaphors can invite us to think of a person as an animal (*he's an absolute pig*), a memory as an action (*the thought of it still wounds me*), a lover as a dwarf star (*Juliet is the sun*), an affair of state as a piece of performance (*it was pure political theatre*), and indeed any other combination you wish. The theatre has, within its technical means, similar flexibility. Old can play young, women can play men, black can play white, wood can play stone, large rooms can play small rooms, a wooden O can play the fields of France, and words can play horses printing their proud hoofs i'th'receiving earth.

The means of theatrical production are metaphors for
the worlds they represent. Metaphor is not limited [. . .]
by any notion of *resemblance*.[3]

Following through the logic of this position, Rebellato
suggests that those forms of theatre which attempt, unthinkingly,
to present scenes and events that look very much like their
real-world equivalents, are sacrificing much of the medium's
creative potential: 'we might say that naturalism is a kind of
dead metaphor', he notes.[4] That is, the conventions of naturalism
have become so overly familiar that – like phrases such as 'stick
your neck out' – we just take them for granted, and don't even
think of them any more *as* metaphorical. By contrast, a new
or surprising use of metaphor ('put your dick on the table') or
theatrical convention (a pencil case as bully) can enliven and
compel our imaginative engagement – involving us actively in
negotiating the relationship between what is presented to us and
what it might be *felt* to *mean*.

Crouch's second play, *An Oak Tree*, took the core ideas
explored in *My Arm* another step – by introducing to the stage a
second actor who has neither seen nor read the play in advance.
He or she is literally invited out of the audience at the beginning
of the play (after some reassuring words backstage beforehand),
and we witness thereafter the attempts of this person to navigate
a way through playing a role that has not been rehearsed. Crouch
himself, as the lead performer, gives this actor pieces of script
to read, and various verbal instructions (again, the facts of the
theatrical process are laid completely bare, with no attempt at
'illusion'), and the actor must find a way into playing 'the father'
in the story presented – a man pole-axed by grief at his teenage
daughter's recent death in a road accident. The miraculous
thing is that audiences very quickly come to 'believe' in this
person as Andy, the father – despite all the glaring evidence to
the contrary – and to feel something of his grief. This surprising

3 Dan Rebellato, 'When We Talk of Horses: or, What do we see when we
see a play?' *Performance Research*, Vol. 14 No. 1 (March 2009), p. 25.
4 Ibid., p. 27.

metaphorical substitution (unprepared actor as grief-stricken parent) provides a clear demonstration of Crouch's conviction that the onstage transformation of an actor into an emotionally plausible character is accomplished *in the minds of spectators,* rather than by any virtuosic ability on the actor's part. Arguably, moreover, it is the initial uncertainty and even 'lostness' of the second actor that helps us 'feel' the father's grief so intensely: we empathise with her from the outset (how would *we* feel to be up there not knowing the script?), and we can interpret her very real loss of bearings in relation to the fictional father's traumatised bewilderment.

Crouch's plays, as this instance should demonstrate, are very far from being merely 'theatre about theatre'. Yes, there are complex presentational strategies at work, which are often inspired by the playwright's interest in visual and conceptual art (*An Oak Tree* responds directly to Michael Craig-Martin's 1973 gallery installation of the same name).[5] Yet his various manipulations of metaphor and stage situation always point towards vital, dramatic questions about the things we *value* – both culturally and personally. Most significant artists have a central, insistent concern around which their work tends to revolve, and this, it seems to me, is Crouch's. With *An Oak Tree,* for example, we are invited to consider the implications of the father's imagined transubstantiation of a roadside tree into 'Claire' – his daughter who died at this same spot. Is this the act of a man in denial about his loss, who fails to see reality 'for what it is' – thereby grotesquely mis-valuing the tree? Or is this, conversely, an intuitively creative act by a man engaged in a redemptive process of mourning and healing – whose attentions invest the tree with immense new value? Little in Crouch's work is 'what it appears to be', after all. We are all the time being invited to bring new thoughts and values to bear on the seemingly mundane or familiar, to see simple things in a potentially transformative new light.

5 For a detailed discussion of Crouch's affinity with conceptual art practice, in relation to *My Arm* and *An Oak Tree,* see my journal article 'Authorizing the Audience: The Conceptual Drama of Tim Crouch', in *Performance Research,* Vol. 19 No. 1 (March 2009), pp. 65-76.

We are also, however, consistently asked to question *distorted* values. In *My Arm,* the boy with the arm above his head eventually finds a sense of self-worth through the creative attentions paid to him by a portrait artist, yet this 'redemption' comes too late to save him. His curiosity value as a freak has made him too valuable to others, as a cultural commodity, for timely medical attention to have been sought. Like many young people, the boy seems to suffer from a kind of existential crisis of value and meaning in his own life. Yet instead of finding support and guidance, he is constantly judged by others (relatives, teachers, doctors, artists) in terms of their own assumptions about bad behaviour, mental ill health, or cultural transgression. The boy goes along with all this 'out of nothingness, really'. Meanwhile, through the very process of bringing our own responses to bear on the storyteller and his tale, we too – as audience members – risk becoming implicated in this same, dangerous process of (mis)judgement.

The active involvement of audiences in Crouch's critique of distorted values becomes more direct, and more discomforting, in *ENGLAND* and *The Author*. Both were written to be performed in particular locations – the former in white-walled galleries, the latter at London's world-famous new-writing theatre, the Royal Court – and in both Crouch obliges spectators to ask themselves difficult questions about the cultural institutions they are situated in.[6] In *ENGLAND,* we are welcomed enthusiastically to the gallery by Crouch and his fellow performer Hannah Ringham, as if they are gallery guides and we, the standing audience, are a tour group. We are made very conscious of our physical presence in the gallery – this pristine, temple-like space which lends the art objects housed within it a quasi-religious value. As the play develops, though, it becomes clear that the central character is strangely absent: the two actors alternate lines in a long monologue, as if they are the same person, leaving us uncertain as to whether this person is male or female, gay or straight. The

---

6 For a detailed analysis of these plays and the way they interrogate their staging contexts, see my journal article 'Materialising the Audience: Tim Crouch's Sight Specifics in *ENGLAND* and *The Author*', in *Contemporary Theatre Review,* Vol. 21, No. 4 (2011), pp. 445-463.

only thing we can be fairly certain of is that this character – unlike the eternally preserved artefacts on the walls – is dying. He or she is betwixt and between life and death, neither here nor there, and thus not fully present with us.

The ramifications of all this are brought home to us in the play's second act, as the narrator – now saved from death and invested with a name, 'English' – travels to an unidentified city in the Middle East (or, another room in the gallery). English has come to thank, with a gift of priceless art, the widow of the heart donor whose generosity has saved his/her life. Yet it transpires that the widow believes the heart was stolen, and her comatose husband effectively murdered, so that English might live. *ENGLAND* is a ruthlessly satirical exploration of Western presumptions and privileges, in a globalized world order, and we the audience are implicated directly in its critique by being cast, collectively, in this single role of the veiled Muslim woman. (The actors insistently address us as if we are she, often making extended eye contact with individual spectators.) If, as Western theatregoers, we find ourselves feeling awkward or unsure about having been cast in this 'alien' role, then we also have little choice but to reflect on where we *do* stand in relation to the unsettling questions that the play poses.

With *The Author,* Crouch goes one step further still. Anyone attending this most controversial of his plays has become – by virtue of simply being a theatregoer – its central object of scrutiny. Placed on two banks of directly facing seating, without a stage area in between to divide them, spectators find themselves looking across the divide and watching each other's varying reactions in response to the twists and turns of the narrative. The play's four actors sit amongst the audience, and often address individual spectators directly – even inviting verbal responses. Thus, while most theatre treats the audience as a single, collective mass (and *ENGLAND* casts it as a single person!), *The Author* differentiates its spectators into a range of individuals with identifiable faces and even names. We are made acutely aware that our own responses may differ significantly from those of others, and – since the situations recounted by the actors alternate between being very funny and deeply disturbing – we may well also find ourselves wrongfooted, laughing at things that are really not funny, or upset by the apparent reactions of others.

The Author tells the story of another, fictional play that Tim wrote and directed, that Vic and Esther acted in, and that Adrian saw as an audience member. This other play, we learn, was critically celebrated for its graphically 'real' depiction of a father's violent abuse of his daughter, as set within a wider dramatic landscape of bloodshed in a war-torn Eastern European country. As in *ENGLAND,* then, a troubled 'elsewhere' is referenced within the 'here and now' of the play, but this time we do not travel overseas through the magic of theatre. Instead, the spectre of violence and cruelty has been brought to theatregoers where they sit: it has been translated into theatrical 'art' via a process of creative research that seems to have left the actors themselves traumatised. Who is this fictional 'author', this 'Tim Crouch', who would delve into such darkness for the sake of theatrical entertainment? But equally, who are the spectators that would value such a thing, taking voyeuristic interest in the evocation of real world suffering? Are they, in fact, spectators not unlike those of us sitting here in this auditorium, for this play? To what extent are we accountable for what we choose to watch? It is striking testament to the dramatic power of *The Author* that, at the end of performances, audiences rarely – if ever – applaud. It seems that, rather than submitting to the familiar, habitual ritual of clapping (the dead metaphor of thanks), most spectators would rather be alone with their own thoughts and feelings. The end of the performance is not the end of the story.

Perhaps it is in such personal re-valuations that hope lies. And perhaps, on the other hand, corruptibility lies most readily in contexts where we hand our responsibility for individual judgement over to collective opinion, or to supposed experts and specialists, allowing them to determine what is valuable *for* us. Returning, finally, to my opening anecdote, we might ask what it would have meant for me to do as John Lion suggested, and assert that Shepard was more important than anyone since O'Neill? All it would really have meant, surely, was that I thought my 'dick' was big enough to get away with the assertion. Such declarative judgments are always more about the critic's perceived authority than about anything intrinsic to the artwork. And insofar that we defer to such judgments, and treat them as statements of 'truth' (did you accept my opening claim about Crouch?), we also rob ourselves of our own powers of judgment. The true role of the critic, I believe, is to engage and provoke – to draw people into a discussion rather than closing that discussion down with 'authoritative' claims. Crouch's view of the playwright's role appears to be similar: here is an author who works scrupulously – together with his two directors and his co-performers – to hand authority back to audiences. These plays invite us to seek our own responses and value judgements, and to take personal responsibility for what we witness.

Stephen Bottoms
Professor of Drama and Theatre Studies
Workshop Theatre, University of Leeds

MY ARM

My Arm – The Belt Theatre, New York, 2003
© *Francis Hills*

Previewed at the Hayward Gallery, London, 4 February 2003
Premiered at the Traverse Theatre, Edinburgh, 31 July 2003

Performed by Tim Crouch

Co-directed by Tim Crouch and Karl James
(with Hettie Macdonald)
Film by Chris Dorley-Brown

To the memory of John, Dorothy and David Wilson

A NOTE FOR THE AUDIENCE

Read this

My Arm is partly about giving ordinary things extraordinary significance. What it needs is a supply of everyday objects from *you*: the stuff in your pockets, in your bags, your wallets; stuff you carry around; photographs (driver's licences, IDs, travel cards etc.), lucky charms, key rings, badges, toys. Useful things; useless things. Things no bigger than a shoe.

Anything you supply will be treated with care and respect. It will be in view at all times. No conventional magic will be attempted with it – no hammers and handkerchiefs. You will get it back at the end. But the stuff you supply will create a major part of *My Arm*. Please be ready with possible things when they're requested.

Notes

A table. Onto the top of this is trained a camera. A chair by the table. The feed from the camera is shown on a television that sits at the side of the stage.

At the back of the stage, a much larger screen onto which are projected sequences of film. The films described in this text were those used in the original production. They were home cine film from the 1970s, owned and sequenced by Chris Dorley-Brown.

Apart from a doll that represents the performer, the objects and pictures are in no way representational. They should be any kind of object chosen at random. Ideally, they are objects and photos offered up from the audience before the start. All these articles are left, visible but unlit, on the table top, like actors in the wings.

There is a measured, haphazard quality to how these objects are given aesthetic significance by the events with which they become involved.

The performer collects objects from the audience and places them on the table.

I'm going to hold my breath until I die.

The performer takes a deep breath in.

A pause.

All lights out.

Film sequence plays – a boy running – and ends.

Lights up. The performer removes the lens cap from the camera. The doll is revealed – via the camera – on the screen.

This is me. I'm ten years old. I'm big-boned.

Here I am watching TV.

The doll.

Here I am in my trunks.

The doll.

Here I am with my brother.

The doll.

Here I am watching TV again.

The doll.

This is the house we lived in.

The performer presents to the camera one of the objects from the audience.

This is my dad's car.

The performer presents a photo or an object.

This is my mum's car.

The performer presents a photo or an object.

This is our dog.

The performer presents a photo or an object.

At this time my dad –

Another object.

is a salesman for Artificial Fibres. He drives a second-hand beige Mercedes. He is as old as I am now. My mum –

Another object.

is my dad's professional wife. She does fondue. She drinks gin and soda. My brother, Anthony –

Another object.

is older than me. We're a middle-class family living in the middle of the 1970s in the middle of the Isle of Wight, which is a small island off the south coast of England.

The performer starts to pant heavily, moving the doll in time to the breath.

This is me. I'm hyperventilating. It's 1974, and we're having our tea.

The objects cast as the characters, play out the scene, interspersed with panting.

This is my mother.

MOTHER: Leave him. He'll come to his senses. Eat your tea.

This is my father.

DAD: Anthony. Anthony. Sit in. Pick it up. Sit in and straighten up.

This is Anthony's hand.

The hand of the performer.

My Mother again.

MOTHER: Stop pumping your fists. You'll crack your joints. Gordon. Gordon. He's turning white.

> Stop him. Dear god, what have we mrm to
> mermermer...

The doll collapses on to its side.

*

I'm not feeble-minded, if that's what you're thinking. I've kept abreast of things; I can have a pretty good guess at the human condition. Considering I came from where I came from I think I've done quite well. And so the overwhelming question is why? Why end up here, on my side?

The doll is righted, and the focus tightens on its face.

During one of my early visits to the psychiatric profession it was suggested to my mother that, just as the physiological act of smiling can engender feelings of happiness for the smiler, so, perhaps, for me, somewhere in my mind I had decided that performing an action which could, in the half light, be considered at least intriguing, might engender sensations of intrigue in me.

Or perhaps it's all arbitrary.

My dad would say that it all started at the age of four when, through what he insists to have been an act of will, I didn't move my bowels for over a month. I absorbed enough of my own toxins to kill a horse. Or a Shetland pony, at any rate. He says that the look of triumph on my little face, as they administered the enemas and the suppositories, was the same look that I displayed on the front cover of *Art Monthly* however many years later.

If that was the first display of my 'self-determination', then I was too young to remember the detail of the will behind it. For that moment, we have to go to the Great Silence of 1973.

A silence far longer than is bearable. Eventually broken by:

You'll appreciate how it must have been for all involved.

I don't know what made me such a...cunt.

27

Presents mother object to the camera.

MUM: Daddy's away 'til Thursday. I'm out 'til eight.
            There's cottage pie, Anthony. Gas Mark 6.
            Twenty minutes. Tinned peas. Here's ten
            pence for sweets. That's pudding, or there's
            fruit. Mr. Martin's coming round to look at
            the boiler. Don't disturb him. *His* son's in the
            cadets. *And* he does Judo.

I'm being ruthless in the editing of my material. Thirty years
into an hour. One year every two minutes. It's Mr Martin's
son, Simon, whose name is on the leaflets, who's sitting at
the back now, whose idea this all was, who doesn't do Judo
anymore. Who's looking at his watch.

*

And to start with, it wasn't just me. Anthony was just as bad,
although he denies it now of course. If anything, he was
worse. As the eldest, he led the way and I, like so often then,
just followed along behind, undetermined, indeterminate.
Anthony kept a piece of gum in his mouth throughout the
forty days of Lent. I held a pebble that I'd picked off the
beach at Littlehampton in my mouth for a month. Whenever
we travelled anywhere in the car Anthony and I would see
who could keep their thumbs inside their fists for longest. We
would test each other to see how long we could live on tip-toe,
how long we could go without weeing, how long we could
make our wees last. Anthony discovered that he could turn
his eyelids inside out. I would put needles into the skin on my
palms. Anthony once had to see a doctor after having worn a
rubber band around his finger for a week and a half.

And then there were the silences. If we'd turned our attention
towards more purposeful pursuits then perhaps none of this
would have happened. But then you would never have heard
of me. You might have been spending these moments of your
life doing something else.

One evening, when I was ten and Anthony 14, we had fireworks.

All lights off. A sparkler lit and burns down. Lights up.

My parents had invited the Martins over for the fireworks. It was summer so it must have been late. Their son, Simon –

Another object.

was with Anthony and me in the gazebo at the bottom of our garden. I remember not being able to get comfortable. Simon was more Anthony's age and they talked easily.

The scene is presented with the doll and objects.

SIMON:	Four.
ANTHONY:	No.
SIMON:	Yeah. Four.
ANTHONY:	Who?
SIMON:	Lorraine Dodds. Phillippa Pearce. Carol Payne. Vanessa Doyle.
ME:	Groovy.
SIMON:	Michelle Stevens.

And we had to smell his fingers.

ANTHONY:	Me-smell Stevens.
ME:	Cool.
ANTHONY:	Shut up, spastic.

So, the fireworks over, my brother drifting off, my parents settling into another bottle of rose, I took myself to my room and –

The performer raises the doll's arm up above its head, where it stays until the end.

And that, really, is the beginning, the middle and the end.

*

Apart from Anthony, no one noticed for the first day. That night I stood in front of the mirror on the landing. I took myself to bed and put myself lower down on the bed. I think I thought that the day had been an interesting test and would soon be forgotten.

The next day there was nothing to do. Nothing was planned. The muscles in my shoulder reminded me of what I'd done the day before and I felt a small tremor of excitement about the prospect of doing the same thing again. Instead of going down to breakfast I positioned myself against the headboard of my bed with my arm resting up in the crook of the wall. Very quickly I passed through the threshold of any pain and the discomfort became a little hypnotic. I unbuttoned my pyjama top and looked at the shape of my armpit leading down into the folds of my stomach and up into the tapering of my wrist. Eventually my mother came into my room. I told her, as it was the summer holidays, I was going to spend the day in bed. She was happy to be free of me for the day. In the evening I came down quietly and placed myself on the sofa to watch TV. That night I woke, aware that I had moved up the bed and brought my arm down. I got up and made a simple cuff which I attached to the headboard. I was then able to sleep with my hand resting in the cuff, my shoulder twisting up from the pillow.

The next day my father was home. Still, I think, my mother hadn't really noticed me. When dad asked what I was doing she looked as curious as him. I said that I had pins and needles and that it was greatly relieved if I held my arm up. By the fourth day the burning in my shoulder was unbearable. I thought that enough was enough and that was that. I felt elated by what I had achieved but, when I brought my arm down, I was swamped by a feeling of failure. Also, the pain was as bad now with the arm down as it was up. I had clearly reached a halfway mark, where I could go either way. I decided to try another day of it. It was nearly the weekend; if I could get to Saturday then that would be a marker.

Friday was complicated by the fact that I had to go to my aunts. Mum was concerned that my pins and needles should be lasting so long. I told her it was feeling much better and spent most of the day either leaning against walls or watching TV.

In the car I rode home with my arm out of the open window and felt like a super hero. It felt like it would take more effort to live with my hand down now than up.

The following Monday my dad bellowed at me, slapped my face, shook me and took me to the doctors. Within a month I had been appointed my very own child psychiatrist.

I was the boy with the arm.

*

The performer writes the words 'Mrs Williams' on a card and places an object next to it.

MRS WILLIAMS: Is there anything you want to say about what we talked about last week?

Do you remember what we talked about last week? Have you thought more about why you're doing what you're doing and how it upsets your mummy and daddy? Your mummy had a cry, didn't she? Why don't you stop it now and make your mummy happy.

Mrs Williams suggested that my action was a plea for attention. She said that everyone feels better about themselves if they feel that they are being noticed, but that in this modern world it was easy to feel invisible. She gave me a small doll to keep –

An object is held up where it can 'see' the performer.

and said that if ever I was lonely or on my own, that I should set the doll up somewhere where it could see me, and then I would feel I was being noticed, and that what I was doing was appreciated by somebody else. This way I would feel that I had less to prove and that maybe one day I would want to put my arm down and get on with things like a normal ten-year-old.

The object is replaced.

I can't begin to describe my sense of definition and power. I realised for the first time where I ended and the rest of the world began – I felt sharp, delineated. For the first time in my life, the air I breathed had an edge. I was setting the rules. I had a special place in school assemblies so as not to confuse visitors. I was excused PE. I spent break time with the school nurse. I was appointed a social worker. People stared at me in the street. No one knew what was going on. They felt threatened. I became the focus of aggression. I triggered insecurities. In 1977, during the Silver Jubilee celebrations, I was approached by two fathers from the school.

The scene is played out with objects.

MAN 1:   What do you fucking think you're fucking doing?

MAN 2:   Put your fucking arm down you fucking prick.

MAN 1:   Put your fucking arm down or we'll fucking rip it off and stick it down your fucking throat, you fucking freak.

It was the highlight of my life so far.

A slow fight – acrobatic, presented for the camera.

Because the muscles around my shoulder had started to atrophy, and because the bones around the socket of my arm were starting to skew, and because the ball joint had begun to ossify, when they snapped my arm it tore a blood vessel at the base of my neck.

The fight stops. The objects are replaced.

And when the doctors set my arm they had to set it up.

And when they took away the cast, the physiotherapist demanded that I work to bring it down. And when I refused to bring it down my GP referred me to a clinic for children with behavioural problems. And my aunt, who attended a spiritualist church in Ryde, declared that I was possessed, and set about arrangements for an exorcism, and my mother resisted her sister's wishes, but determined that we should all go to church so that I could think about things beyond this world. She thought, I suppose, that, as a family, we ought to explore the transcendent.

And throughout this period Anthony –

Anthony object.

called me wanker.

'Wanker.'

He said I'd stolen his idea and said that it had gone beyond a joke and that I should fucking stop it. And when I said it wasn't his idea, that in fact, it wasn't any idea at all, he would leap on me and threaten to bind my arm, which is not far off what Mrs Williams finally resorted to recommending as a way of breaking my psychosis.

There was a report in the local paper titled 'Armed Assault: Two arrested for assault on arm boy.' It explained how I had become something of a curiosity to local residents, and it showed a photograph of my dad. The court case stirred up a lot of atmosphere at home. Looking back on it, I think my mother was undergoing a slow process of grief, although both my parents were locked in the stage of denial. Life went on as normally as possible. Dad became head of a sales division. Everyone in the house either started smoking or started smoking more. Everyone in the house either started drinking or started drinking more. Anthony became one of the few punks on the Isle of Wight, which seemed to upset my mother even more than my irritating gesture. The issue of my arm had been subsumed within the domestic routine. It no longer felt like a questionable act of will, but more like a fact of life, like a squint or a pigeon chest. I had pain, but mostly it felt numb, and the numbness was far outweighed by the continuing sense of euphoria. As well as breathing, smoking, drinking, watching TV and occasionally going to school, this was also something that I did. I adapted my life to my circumstances and felt bemused when people or institutions made a fuss. I did as little with my life as I had done before, but now, when I was doing nothing I had a sense that I was also doing something. This balance kept me held, suspended without future or failure. After a few years, when people realised it really wasn't a stunt, I began to feel my stature grow. Girls began to show an interest, if out of nothing more than a kind of ghoulish fascination. I never mentioned my arm. I lost some weight. In 1979, after Anthony's A Levels, we went to the Balearics for a fortnight. On our return Anthony went to London. To art college in London. And I was referred by Social Services to a residential convalescence home for young people who had undergone trauma.

*

As far as I could tell, the purpose of my stay was for members of the psychiatric departments of several universities to work out what the big idea was. I was subjected to a series of tests, lengthy interrogations about my family, my childhood. I was given the opportunity to confront an imaginary cast list from my life through role play. No one actually ever asked me to put my arm down, but clearly they wanted a success, whatever that might mean. I was put in a group of similarly aged adolescents with similarly idiosyncratic manifestations. There were twin girls, Helen and Alison –

The performer presents to the camera a photo provided from the audience.

who had refused to open their eyes since they were nine. Andy Beglin –

Another photo.

34

who would never open his fists. A girl called Barbara Matthews –

Another photo.

who had had the contents of her stomach removed regularly since the age of five because she kept on eating batteries. Myrna Kendall –

Another photo.

who refused to wash or cut her nails or clean her teeth, ever.

There was an even fatter kid than me who had big issues with his own excrement, so we all kept our distance. And there was Kevin Proctor –

Another photo.

who was perfectly sensible but who would never wear any clothes if he could help it. Kevin would parade around the corridors displaying the thickest pubic hair and smallest penis I had ever seen on a boy of 14.

Like a peanut –

Presents a peanut.

on a bird's nest.

Presents a bird's nest.

*

In all their investigations into the nature of my trauma I remained unruffled. I didn't see what I had to offer. I got the sense from my parents that they were relieved to have their offspring off their hands. They were busy with their lives, and I don't remember not being busy with mine.

Anthony was busy enough with his. He was squatting a house in New Cross with several friends. Every now and then he would send me a postcard that he'd made himself with details of his new life. One vacation he came home and took a series of photographs of my face. He glued the photos onto a canvas and then painted over them with whitewash. He told me that he'd taken letters that I had written to him, burned them and then displayed the ashes between two plates of glass. He said on the course they were exploring representations of nothingness. This all seemed a little heavy-handed, but I was flattered that he'd felt the need.

At some point, Simon Martin –

Presents Simon object.

who had failed his exams and had spent a year in Newport taking drugs, went to live with Anthony in his squat. Simon earned money working in a petrol station and spent the rest of his time pretending to be an art student with my brother. Simon, then as now, was distinguished by a ruthless disregard for protocol. Together, he and my brother bulldozed their way through the London scene. Private showings at the ICA, the Serpentine, Waddingtons; New Romantic gatherings in Camden and the West End. Simon operated by the rubric –

The performer writes laboriously on a placard: 'Art is anything you can get away with'. *This placard remains visible to the audience for the rest of the performance.*

Anthony sent me photographs of graffiti they had done on the walls of the National Gallery, descriptions of junk installations they had built in their squat, photographs of women he had slept with. I walled myself up in my bedroom. The psychiatrists had washed their hands of me. The only formal attention I received was from the medical profession who were concerned that, if I continued the way I was, I would start to lose my fingers. Already by the age of 16 my hand was blackening from lack of blood and most of my fingernails had fallen off. Doctors were worried that the flesh on my arm would become necrotic and, in fairness, on a hot day, the smell was sometimes unavoidable close up. My one concession was to occasionally wear an elasticated mitten, but, by and large, I didn't give it much thought.

*

Excuse me.

A *drink of water.*

On December 24th 1982, outside a bus stop in Ryde, my mother fell down dead.

Film sequence plays – a woman walking into the sea, watched by a child – and ends.

I returned to the family home.

At the funeral dad lost it completely. He was drunk and roared at Anthony and me about how ashamed he was of us both, about how unhappy we had made our mother and that we were probably the cause of her death.

I left home and went to live with Anthony and Simon and a girl called Carla in a new squat near Hackney Marsh. When I arrived in Hackney Simon had got hold of the carcass of a horse from an abattoir and he and Carla were busy stripping the remains of the sinews and bleaching the bones. They had no idea what they were going to do with it, but it had only cost a tenner. In the end the project was ditched, but the house smelt of rotting horse for – well for as long as we were there, which was nearly five years.

My arrival in London made me aware of just what kind of a figure I cut. My mum had adapted most of my clothes so I could put them on easily and, unconsciously, she had hit the style of the time. I was still overweight, but sunken eyes and pale skin seemed to be the fashion. In Hackney I had a room of my own, a portable black and white TV and a corner shop which meant I rarely had to travel far except to sign on and collect my benefit. Anthony provided me with a regular supply of soft drugs, cigarettes, pornographic magazines and fizzy drinks. He busied himself welding kinetic sculptures in the garden. He had moved away from being jealous of me and now cast an over-protective net around my movements. I continued much as I had done on the Island.

Here I am watching TV.

The doll.

Here I am reading pornography.

The doll.

Here I am watching TV again.

The doll.

Years passed like this.

For long stretches of time I would draw the curtains, switch off the lights and sit in the darkness.

All lights out. Complete dark.

Lie on my bed. Stroke my arm. Move about. Get comfortable. Feel myself. Move over here. Stand here like this. Or like this. There was an exquisite sense of abdication, listening to life outside the house. Listening to Carla and Anthony talking, friends coming by, music, doors closing. An older woman called Sue took an interest in me. She was 31 and overweight like me, an actress who worked for a temping agency. One afternoon in the dark Sue took her clothes off and lay down next to me. We both lay very still. I was wearing a black and red striped Mohair sweater. My hair was long; down to here, or here, unwashed. I think Sue thought I would say something important. I held my breath. Sue became upset and whispered things to me I couldn't hear.

Whispering, becoming increasingly insistent.

Whispering stops.

Sue got dressed and left. I watched a re-run of Blakes 7, relieved that she had gone.

Lights up bright.

When I was 22 I became officially registered as disabled. Bits of me kept breaking down, and then they were fixed. I was in and out of hospitals with various blood infections. My lung collapsed. I lost weight. At one point a doctor suggested that if I wanted to live a normal life I would have to have the arm amputated. It was as though he was proposing I murder someone. I was over 21 so no one could force me unless I was sectioned. But nobody sectioned me, although people often talked about it. I conceded to having this finger removed –

The performer presents their finger.

because it was dead. My blood pressure was 180 over 130.

*

Excuse me.

A drink of water.

Anthony's art had moved a long way from representations of nothingness. Tired of welding bits of scrap which nobody wanted, he became involved in a community dark room and presented a small exhibition of photographs showing the detritus left by the police charge at Orgreave during the miners' strike. Carla flirted with being a performance artist, before moving to Cornwall where she became a teacher. Simon left the house and went to live in Pimlico with a Slade graduate called Erica. Through Erica, whose father was an art dealer, Simon got invited to go to Berlin to work as the studio assistant to a very famous German Neo-Expressionist who liked to put horrible and disturbing things in glass boxes and sell them here for thousands of dollars.

When Simon came back from Berlin he asked me if I would work with him on an exhibition that he was planning. It was called *Man-i(n)festation* –

The performer writes the word on a card and presents it to the camera.

with a hyphen after the 'Man' and brackets around the 'n' of 'in'. *Man–i(n)festation. Man-i(n)festation.* And it was all about me. I was even in it. I went along with it all out of – out of nothingness really. Simon's idea was, I think, that I was a bit of an oddity. He took photographs of me, naked. Naked sitting on my bed. Naked in the bath. Naked by the stump of a tree in Erica's garden. I felt like Kevin Proctor.

The performer re-presents the photo from earlier.

He photographed me clothed and out and about, signing on, outside a newsagent. By each photograph that was displayed in the exhibition were descriptions of social and military injustices made to look like my medical records. One room contained huge lithographic reproductions of the texture of my arm and hand with titles such as *Death (in Life)*. Another had a smaller collection of double exposure Polaroids with healthy arms superimposed on images of me sleeping, as though I were dreaming about arms. The centrepiece of *Man-i(n)festation* was me, sitting in a cradle for three two-hour shifts each day, watching television through ear phones. Bulgarian chants were piped through the gallery. I should have enjoyed the attention, but didn't feel able. *Man-i(n) festation* was a great success. *Death (in Life)* was bought by a Harley Street plastic surgeon for £2500. Simon gave me £200. A journalist called Chris wrote a piece about *Man-i(n) festation* which was published in a small art magazine. He praised Simon's 'textural acuity' and recommended Simon's 'nominative effectualism' as a way of 'eliding the dualistic conceits of conception and perception.' Even though the gallery was in Barnet, Simon made sure that everyone who should see *Man-i(n)festation* saw *Man-i(n)festation.* He sold some of the polaroids, a couple of the prints and spent several months trying to interest publishers in producing a book of the exhibition.

Anthony didn't see *Man-i(n)festation*, but wrote an angry letter to the gallery. He was working for a Refugee Action organisation encouraging refugees to document their experiences through collage.

*

I told Anthony that I now wanted to move home to the Island.

Not having cried for as long as I could remember, I had now taken to crying like a new-born lamb looking for its mother in the rain.

*

Dad had married again – a woman called Barbara.

The performer presents a photo or an object.

I was too ill to go to the wedding and Anthony had decided to stay and look after me. A few months later Dad came to London on business and the three of us attempted some kind of reconciliation in a wine bar in Finsbury Park.

The father and Anthony objects sit in silence with the doll. Moved into different configurations. Increasingly frantic. Silence.

Dad took me home.

Barbara hated me. Hated Anthony. Probably hated Dad. But Dad could now afford to play golf and Barbara loved golf. This was the golden era of daytime, confessional TV and Barbara and I would sit across the lounge from each other drinking sherry, smoking Dunhills and watching a trail of battered lives parading before us. Barbara's initial tactic towards me was a kind of warped maternalism – suggesting activities, therapies. She even once asked me if I'd like to help her bake a cake.

Being back in the family home again induced none of the intensity or comfort I'd hoped for. Dad behaved as if I wasn't there. He'd become thick with Mr Martin –

One of the same objects from the Silver Jubilee fight is presented.

which, after the Silver Jubilee incident and the court case seemed a bit rich. They played golf together and Mr Martin would regale my Dad with tales of his own son's success in the London art scene. Simon was now curating a small gallery in Bethnal Green and displaying bits of his own work in a gallery here. This only fuelled my Dad's resentment of me. I had become a totem of all that was wrong with the younger generation. And I was nearing 30.

*

I tried to kill myself by taking Barbara's car and driving it into a tree. As I couldn't drive, I couldn't get up sufficient speed but a set of golf clubs in the back seat ruptured my spleen and I had to have an operation. You can see the scar.

The performer lifts up their shirt to show their back.

When I came out of hospital Barbara said it was the last straw. She said I stunk out the house and that I would have to leave. Dad was looking into residential care homes when Simon Martin phoned.

The scene is presented with the Simon object and the doll.

SIMON:	It's Si.
ME:	Hello.
SIMON:	What are you up to?
ME:	How's Erica?
SIMON:	Brilliant.
Me:	Right.
SIMON:	I have a suggestion.
ME:	Right.

And Simon told me of a famous painter whom Erica had befriended. This famous painter had seen photographs of me and felt she wanted to use me as a subject. I told Simon that I had nowhere to live. He said that he and Erica had bought a flat in St Catherine's Dock, that there was a spare room and that I could come and live with them if I wanted. I said I didn't know what I wanted. Simon said he would act as my manager; he would look after me.

The famous painter's studio was in Notting Hill Gate. She painted at night; she would need me to sit over a period of at least nine months as and when; she would pay me £8,000. She also offered to pay for a taxi to get me back and forth from Simon's flat. She offered to show me some of her other paintings, but I said I wasn't interested. She told me that she liked to paint people naked and asked if I would mind taking my clothes off.

*

The performer picks up the doll and holds it against their chest.

Those nine months were the beginning of my life. Nine months felt right; it was a gestation, and the finished painting was my re-birth. On the first night she got me to stand in the middle of her studio, legs slightly apart and to look just past her. My hair was shorter than it is now, but we took it out of its pony tail and it rested on my shoulders. I kept my glasses on. I can't see without my glasses. And that was it. She looked at me for half an hour, moving around me, and then we rested and talked. Then another half an hour and she made some lines. Then she asked me to look directly at her, to stand in a similar position but to put slightly more weight onto one leg. Half an hour looking, half an hour resting and then more lines on the paper. She said she was looking for my composition. At three in the morning she opened a bottle of wine. We drank it, she ordered a taxi and I went home. Two days later she called me and the process continued.

We worked under a bright naked light bulb. There was no refuge or pretence. She hid nothing of what she was doing from me. She didn't want me to pose, but just to be. As soon as my concentration wavered, if I thought about other things, then she knew it immediately and we rested. It was a feat of endurance for both of us. I felt illuminated – as though her focus was a searchlight that picked me out. Sometimes she asked me to talk about my life. Sometimes she just did sketches of my arm as I sat on a sofa. Sometimes she wouldn't call me for over a month as she was working on another painting. Sometimes I couldn't see her because I was attached to a drip. My blood pressure was 200 over 150.

We worked together on four canvasses over four years – plus a sheaf of sketches, line drawings, charcoals.

I felt redeemed. I felt meaningful like someone other than yourself is meaningful. For the first time ever I wished I could retract everything, go back, counsel myself out of myself on that night with the fireworks. Bereavement and redemption in the same breath.

The paintings won awards. I became renowned. People wanted to meet me. I was too ill to do anything, but I became observed, which perhaps is all that anyone other than yourself can hope to be. There were articles and interviews. Channel Four asked to make a documentary. This is probably where you start to come into the story. Other artists made approaches but Simon took control. He and Erica started to make casts of my arm. Two bronzes were made. One is in the Hirshhorn Gallery in Washington, DC –

The performer presents an object or a photo.

The other is on permanent loan to the Musée National d'Art Moderne at the Centre Georges Pompidou in Paris.

The performer presents an object or a photo.

There are maquettes of my arm in Madrid,

The performer presents an object or a photo.

London,

The performer presents an object or a photo.

Birmingham England,

The performer presents an object or a photo.

and here.

*

A drink of water.

Anthony was living with a South African girl called Kim in a house in Stoke Newington. He was organising an exhibition of refugee art for a studio in Hammersmith and spending much of his time writing evaluation reports to the Arts Council. Kim was pregnant, but Anthony offered me a room in the house if I wanted it. I said I didn't know.

I suggested to Simon, however, that now would be a good time to stop what I had started twenty five years before. A consultant at Guy's Hospital had suggested that some of my medical ills could be remedied if the arm, much of the shoulder and my right lung were removed. He offered his services and described the operation and what it would leave me with.

The performer draws a diagram on a notepad, marking a line and scoring through where the arm would be removed.

Simon was resistant. He wanted to take me to the States. I couldn't fly because of the danger of thrombosis, but Simon offered to pay for a trip across the Atlantic by boat. Erica's father was friends with the foremost American art dealer who was interested in meeting me. Simon urged me to consider putting off any operation until after we'd met. He said that this man had single-handedly resurrected the US market in modern art; he owned three galleries here in Manhattan, two in Los Angeles and one in Washington DC; he determined market values; he could make or break an artist's career. Simon was persuasive. The US art world was clamouring to see me, he said. And after all he had done for me, we took a boat trip to New York. Anthony came to wave me goodbye. This boat was nothing like the Isle of Wight ferry.

*

We arrived here in the summer of 2008. When I got off the boat the heat and humidity hit me and I collapsed. I was taken to a hospital on the Lower East Side where they did tests. I was something of a curio to the doctors and nurses.

An English curio. Over the course of my life, they said, I had diseased my heart. Diseased it beyond repair. I was too weak to undergo any surgery. Even amputation would be locking the stable door after the horse had long ago bolted. I was an internal shambles and would probably drop down dead at any moment. At the most I had a couple of years. I had rotted. I had composted from the fingers down. Not surprising really, but odd that one small empty gesture could have had such an effect, and a shame when everything now seemed to be so promising.

In addition to a one-off fee of $250,000, the dealer offered to pay all my medical and living expenses until I died. He would also pay to have most of my body returned to the Isle of Wight for burial. In return I would sell him my arm. Of course he wouldn't take it whilst I was alive, but he would have unrestricted access to my terminal decay – documentary makers, photographers, visual artists. Then, after my death, my arm would be displayed in an aesthetic context to be determined between him, Simon and myself. Any display would be accompanied by an exhibition of my life, including family photographs, cine film, school and medical reports. Simon would oversee the whole package for an undisclosed sum. He would market the run up to my death – television appearances, sponsorship deals, that sort of thing – and he would manage my estate afterwards.

He also arranged for me to give a series of talks about my life.

The performer takes a deep breath in.

A pause.

All lights out.

Reprise of the first film sequence – the boy running – plays and stops.

Lights up bright.

I spoke to Anthony on the phone.

The performer places their head in front of the camera, so that it appears large on the screen.

I said I was sorry that I wouldn't be coming back, but that I'd be more than happy to pay for him to come over. We talked about mum, about the island. Kim was expecting their second child, so he wouldn't be coming over yet, but he would try to in a year or so. He was painting for himself now – small canvasses about his memories. He said he'd send me a portrait he'd done of me as a small boy. In it, he said, I was watching TV, plump and contented. With my arm around him.

The performer replaces the lens cap onto the camera.

Lights out.

The End.

An Oak Tree – Nationaltheater, Mannheim, Germany.
Tim Crouch and a smith, 2005
© *Nina Urban*

EXCERPTS FROM...

an oak tree
1973
objects, water, and text
Collection: National Gallery Of Australia
By Michael Craig-Martin

(There is a glass of water on a shelf. This is an oak tree, a work made by british artist michael craig-martin in 1973. Beside the glass of water there is a text:)

Excerpt 1

Q. To begin with, could you describe this work?

A. Yes, of course. What I've done is change a glass of water into a full-grown oak tree without altering the accidents of the glass of water.

Q. The accidents?

A. Yes. The colour, feel, weight, size...

Q. Do you mean that the glass of water is a symbol of an oak tree?

A. No. It's not a symbol. I've changed the physical substance of the glass of water into that of an oak tree.

Q. It looks like a glass of water.

A. Of course it does. I didn't change its appearance. But it's not a glass of water, it's an oak tree.

Excerpt 2

Q. Do you consider that changing the glass of water into an oak tree constitutes an art work?

A. Yes.

Q. What precisely is the art work? The glass of water?

A. There is no glass of water anymore.

Q. The process of change?

A. There is no process involved in the change.

Q. The oak tree?

A: Yes. The oak tree.

Q: But the oak tree only exists in the mind.

A: No. The actual oak tree is physically present but in the form of the glass of water.

(Reproduced by kind permission of Michael Craig-Martin)

Previewed at the Nationaltheater Mannheim, Germany, 29 April 2005

Premiered at the Traverse Theatre, Edinburgh, 5 August 2005

Performed by Tim Crouch and a second actor

Co-directed by Tim Crouch, Karl James and a smith
Original sound design by Peter Gill

to Pam and Colin

'The distinction between fact and fiction is a late acquisition of rational thought – unknown to the unconscious, and largely ignored by the emotions.'
Arthur Koestler

Notes for the second actor

(Given to anyone who may be considering taking part in a performance.)

An Oak Tree is a two hander. It's a bit over an hour long. I'm the author and one of the actors. As the second actor, you would walk on stage with me at the start with no knowledge of the play you're about to be in. There is a different second actor in each and every performance of *An Oak Tree*. No one ever does it twice. This device intricately and importantly supports the play's fictional story.

As the second actor in performance, you would never be asked to generate words of your own. Everything you say in the play (and everything I say in the play) has been carefully scripted. You would, however, be asked to be 'open'. (I say the play IS improvised, it's just not improvised with words!) This is a different kind of 'play'. Your performance (with words) would be given to you through a variety of devices: by direct and very simple instructions, by me speaking to you through an earpiece, by reading from pieces of script. There is no casting criteria in any traditional sense. All we ask is that you must have neither seen nor read the play, that you're happy (and confident) to sightread, happy to wear an iPod-style ear piece, happy to allow the play to pass through you and be open to it and your instinct. There is never any pressure on you to be 'perfect'; you can do nothing wrong. There's no preparation, no costume, no lines to learn. The second actor can be male or female, and of any adult age.

If you're up for it, then we would meet an hour before the performance. We'd talk through some ideas behind the play and I'd answer any questions. We'd then test levels on a microphone and practise with a separate bit of script to get a sense of sightreading in the space. I then do the rest – guiding you through an hour or so of theatre in which you carry the main fictional narrative. Much of our work in rehearsal has been about making the second actor's experience feel completely supported and successful; there is no element of cruelty or parody whatsoever in this approach. Each actor who has been in *An Oak Tree* has spoken of a sense of liberation in the process.

One caution is that the story of *An Oak Tree* concerns the loss of a child; if this experience is personally close then we would advise against you getting involved.

If you have any questions, please get in touch with me. In the meantime, don't read the play...

Thanks.

Tim Crouch

Notes

Eight chairs, stacked at the sides of the stage. One piano stool in the middle of the stage.

One handheld wireless microphone. **Bold print indicates amplified speech through the microphone.**

An onstage sound system and speakers.

HYPNOTIST. FATHER.

HYPNOTIST in silver waistcoat, cape, etc. FATHER in whatever everyday clothes the actor chooses to wear.

The actor playing the FATHER (the second actor) can be either male or female, and of any adult age. They will be completely unrehearsed in their role, and will walk on stage at the beginning with no knowledge of the play they are about to be in.

At times, the second actor will wear iPhone/iPod headphones connected to a wireless receiver – this enables the HYPNOTIST to speak to the second actor through a microphone without the audience hearing. This script contains examples of instructions to be given by the HYPNOTIST to the second actor. They are given as guidelines, but detailed attention must be given to these instructions to ensure a constant feeling of support and success for the second actor.

Sections of script are prepared on clip boards. At times, the second actor (and sometimes the HYPNOTIST) will read from these scripts.

The Bach referred to in this script is the Aria from the *Goldberg Variations*. It is a flawed rendition: faltering but ambitious, failing to resolve until the very end of the play when it moves into the First Variation.

Prologue

The actor playing the FATHER is sitting in the audience. The HYPNOTIST walks on stage.

HYPNOTIST: Ladies and gentlemen. Good evening/ afternoon. My name is (*the name of the actor playing the HYPNOTIST*). Welcome to (*the name of the venue*).

Would you come up and stand here, please?

The HYPNOTIST invites the second actor out of their seat in the audience and onto the stage.

Ladies and gentlemen. This is X (*the name of the second actor*). X will be performing in the play this evening. X has neither seen nor read it.

X and I met up about an hour ago. I have given him/her a number of suggestions. I've suggested that they enjoy themselves!

But the story is as new to X as it is to you.

Scene 1

The HYPNOTIST hands the FATHER a page of script: 'Could we just read this together you and me?' The second actor reads the part of the FATHER from the script.

HYPNOTIST: Hello!

FATHER: Hello!

HYPNOTIST: Thanks for this.

FATHER: It's a pleasure!

HYPNOTIST: You hope!

FATHER: Yes!

Pause.

HYPNOTIST: How are you feeling?

FATHER: Okay.

HYPNOTIST: Nervous?

FATHER: A little.

HYPNOTIST: It'll be fine. You'll be fine.

FATHER: I'm sure.

HYPNOTIST: Any questions before we start?

FATHER: Not really.

HYPNOTIST: Nothing?

FATHER: How long is the show?

HYPNOTIST: It's just over an hour.

FATHER: Okay.

HYPNOTIST: Anything else?

FATHER: How free am I?

HYPNOTIST:	Every word we speak is scripted but otherwise –
FATHER:	Okay.
HYPNOTIST:	Anything else?
FATHER:	Not really.
HYPNOTIST:	Just say if you feel awkward or confused and we'll stop.
FATHER:	Okay.

The HYPNOTIST takes the FATHER's script from him/her.

HYPNOTIST:	Good.
	Can I ask you just to look at me.
	Ask me what I'm being. Say, 'What are you being?'
FATHER:	What are you being?
HYPNOTIST:	I'm being a hypnotist.
	Look.
	I'm fifty-one years old. I've got a red face, a bald head and bony shoulders. *(This must be an accurate description of the actor playing the HYPNOTIST.)*
	Look.
	I'm wearing these clothes.
	Now ask who you are, say 'And me?'
FATHER:	And me?
HYPNOTIST:	You're a father. Your name's Andy. You're 46 years old, you're six foot two. Your lips are cracked. Your fingernails are dirty. You're wearing a crumpled Gore-tex jacket. Your trousers are muddy, say, your shoes are muddy. You have tremors. You're unshaven.

Your hair is greying. You have a bloodshot eye.

That's great! You're doing really well!

Also, you'll volunteer for my hypnotism act. You'll volunteer because I accidentally killed your eldest daughter with my car and you think I may have some answers to some questions you've been asking. I won't recognise you when you volunteer. I won't recognise you because, in the three months since the accident, you've changed. We've both changed.

Pause.

There.

That's about as hard as it gets, I promise.

Let's face out front. Ask who they are, say 'Who are they?' (*i.e. the audience.*)

FATHER: Who are they?

HYPNOTIST: They're upstairs in a pub near the Oxford Road. It's this time next year, say.

Let's say they're all a bit pissed.

But don't worry, X, they're on your side. It's me they're after.

Face me.

I'm just going to talk to them. I won't be a second.

(*To the audience.*) Ladies and gentlemen. In a short time I'll be asking for volunteers from the audience but I'm not asking you. I'm asking some people in a pub a year from now. So please don't get up.

(*To the FATHER.*) That's them dealt with!

Are you okay? Say 'Yes'.

FATHER: Yes.

HYPNOTIST: Good. Really good.

Let's start. You can put your headphones in, and switch on your pack.

The FATHER puts in their earpiece and switches on the receiver.

We take our time. We're in no hurry.

Would you go and sit back in the audience?

The HYPNOTIST motions the FATHER to their seat in the audience.

Good luck. I'm sure you'll be great.

Three. Two. One.

Scene 2

The HYPNOTIST puts on music. Carmina Burana, 'O Fortuna'. Very loud.

Through the music, the HYPNOTIST arranges chairs into a row across the stage, with the piano stool in the centre. He then visits the actor playing the Father and tells them, 'I'm going to ask for volunteers from the audience. I hope no one will volunteer! You will volunteer, but only when I talk to you in your earpiece. Don't do anything until I talk to you in your earpiece. Just sit back and watch the show. And thanks!'

The HYPNOTIST takes up his microphone.

'O Fortuna' ends.

The HYPNOTIST runs on stage.

HYPNOTIST: **Ladies and gentlemen.**

I will welcoming.

I will.

I.

Welcome you to this –

To my hypnotic world.

To my hypnotic world.

In a short minute's time I will be looking for such certain volunteers to come with and join me here on this chairs these. These volunteers that they're –

Now, when before I ask these some hypnotic volun – superstars to come with join me, there is one are one or two things that I'd like to tell you about hypnotic about hypnosis, about stage hypnosis, about the things you're going to see tonight, ladies and gentlemen, or

rather not rather not rather the things you'll never see in any of my shows.

Firstly. I will never lie to you, ladies and gentlemen. You will see no false nothing false tonight. Nothing phoney. No plants, no actors. The people you will see on stage tonight, ladies and gentlemen, apart from me, are all genuine volunteers!

You will be stars of the stars of this evening's –

Of all my shows all my shows are completely clean, ladies and gentlemen. Nobody will reveal any secrets tonight. In the shy, tonight, nothing nothing nobody will reveal any sexual fantasies tonight. There's no stripping in tonight's show. And there's absolutely no sex in at all in.

Sounds shit, doesn't it.

There is one are two types of peerson who cannot be volun – hypnotised. The first type is anyone who is mentally unstable. If you're mentally unstable please remain in your chair.

There may be some ladies here, ladies here who, ladies who are pregnant. If you are pregnant, congratulations, but please don't voluntise teer for tonight's shy. There may be some ladies who are not pregnant but would like to be. Come and see me after the show and I'll sort you out.

Now, in a few moments –

I've got about ten chairs. Nobody will reveal any secrets and nobody will take their clothes off, but apart from that anything could happen.

Come up ladies and gentlemen and give me a piece of your mind.

I'm going to play some music. While the music's playing, if you have an open mind, if you're a game, you're gain for a a laugh and you're over eighteen, then I'd like you to join me on this these chairs.

I'm going to stepping back.

I'm stepping back to let you come forward.

I'm going to play some music.

I'm just the hypnotist, ladies and gentlemen; you're the stars of the show.

Come up, ladies and gentlemen, and give me a piece of your mind.

Your mind.

Your mind.

The HYPNOTIST switches on cheesy 'come-on-down' music.

Music plays.

No volunteers. If audience members do volunteer, they are gently thanked and guided back to their seats by the HYPNOTIST.

The HYPNOTIST feeds instructions to the FATHER's headphones –

> *'I'd like you to count for five in your head and in your own way, your own time, come up stage and sit on the piano stool facing the audience.'*

With the music still playing, the FATHER 'volunteers' for the show – walking onto the stage and sitting on the piano stool.

The moment is held.

Music stops.

The sound of passing road traffic.

HYPNOTIST: You're by the side of a road now, not far from here.

This is the place where your child was killed. You come here regularly. The truth is you can't keep away. This is the sound of that place. Whenever you hear this sound, that's where you are.

It's six thirty in the morning. You've been here for three hours. It's dark and cold and the air is damp.

You're on the phone. Your mobile phone. You're calling home. You want to speak to your wife. Your wife's name is Dawn. Your younger daughter picks up the phone.

The HYPNOTIST may feed the FATHER the following instruction: 'Don't repeat anything now. Just listen to what you say.'

You say, 'Marcy, Marcia, baby, not now.'

You say, 'Tell mummy it's me, darling, would you? Would you baby?'

A lorry thunders past.

You say, 'Dawn, love, I'm sorry. I'm sorry. I couldn't sleep. Dawn.'

You say, 'I'm weaker. I'm weaker than you.'

You say, 'She's here, love. She's here. I'm with her now.'

It starts to rain. Your face flushes with colour.

You say, 'Dawn. Dawn.'

You say, 'Fuck you.'

The HYPNOTIST offers up his microphone to the FATHER.

Would you say 'Fuck you' into the microphone.

FATHER: **Fuck you.**

A lorry thunders past.

HYPNOTIST: The phone's dead. You're cold in this rain. By this tree.

Dawn will come to get you. In about fifty minutes. Towards the end of the play. She'll bring Marcy. She'll tell you that it's fucking freezing. The two of you will argue. You'll argue about the nature of this piano stool. She'll say, 'It's a tree, Andy, it's just a fucking tree'.

Roadside sound stops as the HYPNOTIST switches on the cheesy music again. The HYPNOTIST turns to an empty chair in the line of chairs.

HYPNOTIST: **Have you ever been hypnotised before, young lady?**

X, come and sit on this chair and then say 'No'.

The HYPNOTIST offers his own microphone to pick up the FATHER's replies.

FATHER: **No.**

HYPNOTIST: **Well there's a first time for everything, isn't there ladies and gentlemen. What's your name, gorgeous? Say Amanda.**

FATHER: **Amanda.**

HYPNOTIST: **That's a beautiful name for a beautiful girl. Isn't she beautiful ladies and** gentlemen? Sit back Amanda, relax and enjoy.

What's your name mate?

The HYPNOTIST turns to another empty chair in the line.

Move to this chair say 'Richard'.

FATHER: **Richard.**

HYPNOTIST: **He's a good looking lad, isn't he, girls. A bit of eye candy for the ladies! Just sit back, Richard, sit back and relax! Great.**

And you sir, what's your name?

Move to this one, say 'Keith'.

FATHER: **Keith.**

HYPNOTIST: **It's Keith Richards, ladies and gentlemen!**

You ever been hypnotised, Keith?

Say 'yeah'.

FATHER: **Yeah.**

HYPNOTIST: **Hey, well you'll know when what well you to do, won't you.**

What's your name, darling?

Sit on this chair and say 'Jacqui'.

FATHER: **Jacqui.**

HYPNOTIST: **A bit nervous, Jacqui? Or maybe just a bit pissed!**

Nothing to be nervous about. Just sit back, relax and enjoy the show.

Sit on the piano stool.

Although, Jacqui, actually, it's him I'd be nervous of. *(Referring to the second actor now on the piano stool.)*

What's your name, mate?

Say, 'Can I have a word?'

FATHER: **Can I have a word?**

HYPNOTIST: **Can you have a word?! Yes, mate, you can have a word! Um, 'Bollocks!' That's a word, isn't it? Got a right one here, haven't we ladies and gentlemen, going to have to keep our eyes on that one!!**

Sit on this chair. A big smile out.

I thought I said no one with a mental illness! What's your name, mate?

Say 'Neil'.

FATHER: **Neil.**

The HYPNOTIST kneels. A gag.

HYPNOTIST: **What's your name, mate.**
Say 'Neil'.

FATHER: Neil.

HYPNOTIST: **Your wife in, Neil?** Say, 'Wanker'.

FATHER: **Wanker.**

HYPNOTIST: Go and sit on the piano stool.

HYPNOTIST: **Right mate. Okay.**

Thank you, Neil, if you'd like to go back into the audience and join your party.

The HYPNOTIST puts 'Neil's' chair over on its side and elicits a round of applause from the audience for 'Neil'.

Ladies and gentlemen, a round of applause for Neil!

I want this show to be a good one. I
really do. I was doing a a a gig just last
week. Everything brilliant. Everyone
hypnotised. Everyone doing everything I
asked them to do.

And just before the end of the show,
just before the end I, er, I slipped off
the edge of the stage, arse over tit. And
the last thing I said before I landed
was 'Fuck me'. Couldn't sit down for a
month. A week.

The HYPNOTIST stops the music.

The sound of the roadside is there.

*The HYPNOTIST talks to the FATHER through headphones – inaudible
to the audience.*

> *'Beautiful. You're by the side of the road again.
> It's a really important place for you. It has a really
> strong emotional charge, this place. When I finish
> speaking, I'd like you to count to five in your head
> and then bring your arms out in front of you, as if
> you're hugging a tree.'*

The FATHER brings out his arms.

A lorry thunders past.

> *'Fantastic. Just keep that position.'*

> *'When you hear music, I want you to slowly,
> slowly lower your right arm until it's as low as it
> can go. And at the same time I want you to slowly,
> slowly, raise your left arm as high as you can.
> You can take about 30 seconds, a long time. Start
> moving your arms when the music begins. Your left
> arm will go up, your right arm will go down.'*

*The roadside sound stops as the HYPNOTIST switches on different music
– hypnotic trance music.*

HYPNOTIST: Now, I'm as as that weight is taking your
right hand down I want to imagine that
on your left hand I'm attaching a helium
filled balloon. There, I'm tying a helium
filled balloon around your left left wrist
and I want you to imagine that your left
arm is getting lighter and lighter and
starting to float up higher and higher
and higher. That's great! Really good.
Lighter and lighter. Fifty times lighter.
Fifty times lighter.

No weight, Ian? Nothing? Not even –
Thank you, if you'd like to go and rejoin
the audience.

The HYPNOTIST puts down another empty chair ('Ian's' chair).

Ladies and gentlemen, a round of
applause for Ian!

The FATHER's arms are getting more extreme.

Eyes closed and just imagine. One arm
getting heavier, the other starting to rise.
Lighter and lighter.

That's it, just let yourself give yourself go
to the to the image of the image that I'm
giving you. And really feel the weight
of the weight and the lightness of the
lightness. Fifty times heavier. Fifty times
heavier –

All right. Great. No balloon, Jacqui?

It's absolutely fine, Jacqui. Only a bit of
fun. If you'd like to rejoin your party.
Ladies and gentlemen, Jacqui!

The HYPNOTIST puts down another chair ('Jacqui's' chair).

Keith, was it? Nothing? As we say in
hypnotism, Keith, if it's not there it's

just not there! Go back to the audience
and rejoin your people. Ladies and
gentlemen, Keith!

The HYPNOTIST puts down another chair ('Keith's' chair).

Aren't they doing well?

*The HYPNOTIST talks to the FATHER through the earphones – inaudible
to the audience.*

'The Hypnotist is going to ask you to put your arm
down, but I don't want you to. Don't put your
arm down until I tell you.'

Now I'm going to pop that balloon and
I'm going to cut that weight, and I want
you now just to bring your arms DOWN.

The HYPNOTIST switches off the hypnotic trance music.

Bring your arms down. That's great.
(To the imaginary other volunteers.) Bring it
down. Bring your arm down, mate. (*To the
FATHER who still has his arm up.*) Alright, and
stop. Stop it. Let's all just stop this, shall
we? Put your arm down.

Now. He's funny, isn't he ladies and
gentlemen? A bit of a joker.

You think you're very funny, don't you.
A night out with your mates, have a
few pints, have a laugh. Fuck around.
We think it's funny, don't we? Don't we,
ladies and gentlemen?

What's your name, mate?

Say 'I can't move my arms'.

The HYPNOTIST picks up the FATHER's replies with his microphone.

FATHER: I can't move my arms.

HYPNOTIST: **Do you think I was born yesterday? Cut it out.**

Say 'Please untie me?'

FATHER: **Please untie me?**

HYPNOTIST: **A right one here!**

You having a laugh at me? Put your arm down, mate.

Say 'I can't move.'

FATHER: **I can't move.**

HYPNOTIST **Stop fucking around. This bit's finished. Isn't it, Shirley? Richard?**

Take your time, look me in the eyes and say, 'Please help me.'

FATHER: **Please help me.**

The moment is held.

The sound of the roadside again.

The HYPNOTIST gives the following instructions directly to the FATHER:

Brilliant. You can relax your arms. You're doing really well. Take your time. Enjoy yourself.

I want you to count to ten in your head, and then stand up.

The FATHER stands up.

The HYPNOTIST talks to the FATHER through the headphones:

'You're by the side of the road again. This is a really important place for you. It's the place where your daughter was killed. And you come here every morning and you watch the cars go by. Here, where you are, by this road.'

> '*Now, in your own time and in your own way, I want you to lie down on the floor in front of you.*'

The FATHER lies down on the floor.

A lorry thunders past.

As the HYPNOTIST instructs the FATHER through the headphones, he puts down three more chairs, until there are just three remaining – including the piano stool.

> '*Brilliant. Now we're going to have some fun! For the moment now, I want you to do exactly what the Hypnotist says. Just follow the Hypnotist's instructions.*'

Hypnotic trance music starts again.

HYPNOTIST: **...on a golden, sandy beach.**

Beautiful. Lovely. Nice and relaxed. Nice and relaxed. Aren't they relaxed, ladies and gentlemen? Feel the warmth of the sun beating down and feel your body sinking in to the nice warm golden sand. That's lovely.

And now, now, I want you to get up off the floor and come and sit back on your chairs on the stage. That's it. All three of you. And now, these chairs aren't your normal chairs, oh no. These are special chairs. These are chairs at the Albert Hall! You're on stage at the Albert Hall. And I'm going to play some different music, and when the music starts all the ladies and gentlemen in the audience want to see you play the piano. Don't we ladies and gentlemen? You're going to play the piano for the ladies and gentlemen. Nod your head if you understand.

The FATHER nods his head.

> **The music's going to play. When it plays
> you're onstage at the Albert Hall and
> you're going to play...the...piano!**

The HYPNOTIST stops the trance music.

*Piano music plays. The HYPNOTIST gives the following instruction to
the FATHER:*

> Keep on playing. Play the piano and really
> get into it, enjoy it. Close your eyes if you
> like. When the Hypnotist says "Sleep"
> that's when you stop. The Hypnotist saying
> "Sleep" is your only cue to stop.

*The HYPNOTIST puts down the remaining two chairs. 'Aren't you going
to play for the ladies and gentlemen, Shirley?' etc. Only the FATHER
playing the piano on the piano stool is left, surrounded by eight chairs
scattered around the stage. The moment is held.*

> **What's he doing, ladies and gentlemen?
> What is he doing? Someone put you up
> to this? Is this a trick, a joke, is it?**
>
> **You're not convincing. You're not
> believable. We can see you're trying
> it on, can't we ladies and gentlemen?
> The show's over, isn't it, ladies and
> gentlemen? A piece of shit wasn't it?
> Couldn't hypnotise a fly, could he? We
> just want to forget about it, don't we,
> turn back to our drinks. Don't you ladies
> and gentlemen? They know this isn't
> a piano, you know this isn't a piano.
> There's no piano there. There was never
> a piano. You can't do this. We don't
> believe you. You can't – You can't. Stop
> it. STOP IT.**
>
> **And sleep.**

The HYPNOTIST stops the piano music.

Bit of a wanker, here, ladies and gentleman. Thinks he's a bit of a star, doesn't he? Friend of yours, is he? Anyone know him? Nobody? Shall we have a bit of fun, eh? See what he's really made of, stop him fucking about. Shall we? Because we all know he's only putting it on, don't we? We all know somebody's put him up to this.

Open your eyes, mate.

Listen, mate. I'm going to count down from three. And when I get to one, you'll get up, you'll look down and you'll see that you're absolutely bollock naked. Completely starkers, in front of all the ladies and gentlemen. Nod your head if you understand.

Nod your head.

And not only that, but when you hear this sound *(The HYPNOTIST makes A fart sound.)* you'll be convinced that you've shat yourself. That warm shit is running down the back of your naked leg. Nod your head if you understand.

And then – And then, when I click my fingers, you'll become convinced you've done something terrible, and you'll feel really guilty – truly terrible, ladies and gentlemen. When I click my fingers, you'll be convinced convinced that you've killed someone. Yeah. You've killed a little girl, a girl, haven't you, and you'll feel really awful. A little girl. Nod your head if you understand.

This should be fun, shouldn't it, ladies and gentlemen. We're looking forward to it, aren't we?

And, three, two...

The HYPNOTIST gives instructions directly to the FATHER.

The Hypnotist is going to humiliate himself more than anyone else in this exchange now. Do what he asks you to do. Your cue to stop is 'Sleep. 'Sleep' is your only cue to stop.

...one.

Music plays. A ghastly, jaunty, clownish music.

Hey, mate, stand up. Oh, where are all your clothes? Eh? Ladies present, mate. Show a bit of respect. And, oh, look at your little chap. Cold out, is it? Where is he, won't he come out to play? That must be a bit embarrassing. Listen to this, mate. Listen to this. (*Makes a farting noise*) Oh, dear, mate, what's happened there, eh? Oh dear, that's a bad smell. Couldn't you have waited? Urgh, all down your leg and all. How do you feel about that? Pretty bad, eh? Pretty apologetic towards me, I imagine. And to everyone. Stinking up the place with your stinky shit. Like you want to say sorry, I should think.

Say 'Sorry'.

FATHER: Sorry.

HYPNOTIST: Louder.

FATHER: Sorry.

HYPNOTIST: Say, 'Sorry for my stinky shit.'

FATHER: Sorry for my stinky shit.

The HYPNOTIST clicks his fingers.

HYPNOTIST: **And what about that kid. A girl was it? Didn't see her coming? What were you doing? You were driving your car, weren't you? Driving along, were you. Drive along. Put your hands on the wheel. Drive. Look at you, you're driving! Turn and wave at the audience as you drive your car along.**

The HYPNOTIST gets the FATHER to mime driving.

She wasn't looking, was she? Maybe she was listening to music, silly girl! Here she is, a little girl, here she is. And there's you in your car. Just stepped out, didn't she. Look out, mate, look where you're going! Look out for that girl. Look out! Oh, and she's dead! You killed her! Think of her little body. Think of her poor mummy and daddy. Just driving along, were you? How does that make you feel? What do you wish you were? I bet you wish you were dead! Say it. What do you wish? You wish you were dead. Say 'I wish I were dead'. SAY IT.

FATHER: **I wish I were dead.**

Louder.

FATHER: **I wish I were dead.**

HYPNOTIST: **What?**

FATHER: **I wish I were dead.**

Keep driving along, keep waving to the audience and keep telling the audience that you wish you were dead until I say 'Sleep'. Keep going, even when the music stops.

FATHER: I wish I were dead, etc.

77

HYPNOTIST: **All right. Enough. Stop. STOP.**
FUCKING STOP THIS.

The HYPNOTIST stops the clownish music. The FATHER keeps driving an imaginary car and keeps saying, 'I wish I were dead'. The moment is held.

And SLEEP.

What are you doing? What's happening?
Why are you doing this to me? What are
you doing here? Why are you here?

Say 'I'm Andrew Smith'.

FATHER: **I'm Andrew Smith.**

HYPNOTIST: Say 'I'm Claire's dad'.

FATHER: **I'm Claire's dad.**

HYPNOTIST: Say 'The girl'.

FATHER: **The girl.**

The Bach piano music plays and stops.

HYPNOTIST: Oh Jesus. Oh God.

An audible instruction is given immediately:

The piano's going to play. I'm going to go
down to my knees now. Just watch me.

The Bach plays. The HYPNOTIST falls to his knees.

Bach stops.

Bach plays. During it, the HYPNOTIST sets up and instructs the FATHER for the next scene.

The HYPNOTIST gives the following instruction:

Great. End of Act One! We're going to read
together now, you and me. I'm going to get
you some script. I won't be a second.

The HYPNOTIST gets the appropriate pieces of script.

We read this directly out to the audience.
Take your time. Make it your own. Feel your
way. We start when the music stops.

Bach keeps playing. Bach stops.

Scene 3

The HYPNOTIST and the FATHER stand side by side. Both read from scripts.

HYPNOTIST: That evening. Dusk.

FATHER: That evening.

Watching Claire leave – her headphones on, sheet music stuffed into a bag. A five minute walk to the lesson.

Dusk.

HYPNOTIST: This was my route. A fiftieth birthday party in a sports hall. I had to phone and cancel. I said there'd been an accident, but I didn't give details.

FATHER: That night. That night has a colour, a touch and a sound. Dawn was back. We waited for Claire. We delayed supper for Claire. We stood at the door for Claire. Marcy was watching The Simpsons.

Blue. We delayed supper in blue. We stood at the door in lilac. We brushed against each other in slate grey. We looked at our watches in yellow. Dusk.

HYPNOTIST: I was driving a Ford Focus estate. 1.6 Litres. The car was good. The brakes were good. ABS. Airbags. In the back, speakers, sound board, microphones, costumes. My lights were on. November.

FATHER: Purple. Our pulses raced in purple. We phoned the piano teacher in brown. Our stomachs knotted in green. The policeman walked up the path in red. We watched him from the window in orange. He took off his hat at the door in gold. White. Dawn's knees gave way in white.

HYPNOTIST: This is the point on the map. This is the Ordnance Survey grid reference. This is the Street View. This is the bend on the road. This is the black spot. These are the leaves by the kerb.

FATHER: Death. Death walked through into the lounge. He put his helmet on the piano stool, spoke to us in silver. He then pronounced two concrete blocks in black and left them to hang inside my ribcage, pushing against my lungs. Where they remain to this day. Recently I asked Dawn if she thought I should go to the doctors to arrange to have them removed. 'Where's my man?' she screamed. 'Where's my fucking husband gone?'

HYPNOTIST: These are the yellow lines, the white lines. This is the quality of the light. This is the tree by the verge. This is the tree. This is the view from the North. This is the view from the South. This is my hand, reaching down for a cigarette. For a second. At 37, 38, 39. Twenty metres. In the dusk. This is the girl. Stepping into the road. Her headphones on. Some piano music. On the way to her lesson.

Bach plays and stops.

Bach plays. The HYPNOTIST feeds the following instructions to the FATHER.

Fantastic. Beautiful. Come and stand here. We're going to go back to that moment when I was on my knees, and we're going to carry on from there.

I'm going to get a bit more script.

The HYPNOTIST gets the appropriate piece of script.

> Now we work together. We act together. We
> start when the music stops.

Bach continues to play.

Scene 4

The HYPNOTIST goes down on his knees – to the position he was in at the end of Scene 2.

The Bach stops.

The FATHER reads from his script. The HYPNOTIST has no script.

HYPNOTIST: Look, let's get out of here. I'll buy you a drink. I had no idea you were –

FATHER: A drink of what? What?

HYPNOTIST: Look. This isn't the best –

We should find somewhere more – Hang on. Let me talk to the audience. I won't be a second.

Ladies and gentlemen.

I'd like to apologise for – If you'd be kind to wait just a few moments, I'm happy to refund your tickets. In the meantime, I can only apologise – Please, this performance is now over. The bar is open.

Look, let me give you my – we can – I need to –

FATHER: I'm sorry.

HYPNOTIST: No, no. It's me. I'm – As you can see, things haven't been going too well. I'm just honouring old bookings. It's not –

FATHER: I need to wipe this up –

HYPNOTIST: What?

Indicate the back of your legs and say 'This'.

FATHER: This.

HYPNOTIST:	I don't understand.
FATHER:	I'm so sorry. I don't know what happened. I need a towel or something, something to cover – In front of all these people. I don't know what happened. It's not like me.
HYPNOTIST:	What?
	Indicate the backs of your legs again and say 'This'.
FATHER:	This.
HYPNOTIST:	No. There's nothing. It was a suggestion. There's nothing there. You didn't –
	You're fully clothed.
	There's no mess there. It was me. I was doing it. I hypnotised you. I put you under.
	I didn't think you'd – I thought nobody had – I thought you were taking the piss. People take the piss. I didn't recognise you. It's been three months since –
FATHER:	No. Look. I'm dirty. I need –
HYPNOTIST:	No. I'm sorry.
FATHER:	Yes. Smell. I feel awful. This is not –
HYPNOTIST:	Yes. Yes. Alright. I'm sorry. You're naked. You have shit down your legs.
FATHER:	Yes. I'm sorry.
HYPNOTIST:	Listen. Listen.
	Here. Let me clean you up. Here, with this cloth.

The HYPNOTIST presents an imaginary cloth to the FATHER.

| | This is the right kind of cloth, isn't it? Say, 'Yes'. |

FATHER:	Yes.
HYPNOTIST:	Soon get you clean.
	Stand here and face straight out.

The HYPNOTIST wipes the back of the FATHER's legs with the imaginary cloth.

	There.
FATHER:	I'm sorry about the girl.
HYPNOTIST:	What?
FATHER:	The girl I killed. What was her name?
HYPNOTIST:	What?
FATHER:	The girl I killed. I was driving. You said. I'm sorry.
HYPNOTIST:	No. No, that was – That was me. You didn't –
	There was no girl.
FATHER:	Yes.
HYPNOTIST:	Yes, there was, but not you. You did nothing. Me. It was me. You did nothing.
	I killed someone. You know that. That's why you're here. Why you volunteered.
FATHER:	I'm sorry. I wanted to enjoy the show. I didn't mean to spoil it for you.
HYPNOTIST:	Please. You didn't. Really. Since November, I –
FATHER:	November?
HYPNOTIST:	Since your daughter's death, I've not – I'm not. I've not been much of a hypnotist.
FATHER:	I saw your poster. I recognised your name. When I saw what you did, I was interested. I thought you could help. Will you help? I need help.

My wife – Dawn – she's very unhappy.

I'm so sorry about this.

HYPNOTIST: It's fine. These things happen. It's not your fault. Here.

The HYPNOTIST takes away the FATHER's script.

Now you're clean. Look, see. Clean. The smell has gone. Has the smell gone?

Say 'Yes'.

FATHER: Yes.

HYPNOTIST: Good. That's really good.

Face me.

Now I'm going to put some clothes on you. They're probably not your choice of – I mean, these are just things I've – But let's get you covered up.

The HYPNOTIST starts to clothe the FATHER with imaginary clothes.

Legs in. That's it. Well done. These are good trousers, aren't they? Say 'Yes'.

FATHER: Yes.

HYPNOTIST: There was no girl you killed. No girl. Do you understand? No girl.

It was a game. I was being stupid. I was angry.

Arms out. That's it. This is a nice shirt, isn't it? It's green, isn't it? Yes? Say 'Yes'.

FATHER: Yes.

HYPNOTIST: And this pattern, it's good, isn't it? Say 'Yes'.

FATHER: Yes.

HYPNOTIST: Good. All dressed now. All better now? Yes? Say 'Yes'.

FATHER: Yes.

The HYPNOTIST hands the script back to the FATHER.

HYPNOTIST: We're going to go from here. From my line. 'You're all clean and put back together.'

You're all clean and put back together.

FATHER: Yes, I'm all put back together.

HYPNOTIST: Let's get you home.

FATHER: No.

HYPNOTIST: But –

FATHER: I wanted to see you. I wanted to talk to you at the – since the funeral. But I didn't know how to find you. I wanted to say something.

HYPNOTIST: Andrew.

FATHER: Andy.

HYPNOTIST: Andy,

There's really nothing I – At the inquest, I – It wasn't my fault. Your daughter was listening to music. She didn't – I –

FATHER: No, it's not like that. I'm not here because – I wanted to – I needed you to know. It's good news. It's good news.

Claire's fine.

HYPNOTIST: What do you mean?

FATHER: She's fine. I mean she's okay.

She's not okay.

I mean I found her –

I haven't found her.

I mean I know where she is.

I don't know where she is.

87

Only.

You have to help me.

I've done something.

Something impossible.

And I don't know how I did it.

Something miraculous.

But it's not good.

It's no good.

And I don't know what to do.

I don't know what to do.

Will you help me?

Bach plays.

The HYPNOTIST gives the following instructions directly to the FATHER.

Beautiful. I'm going to feed a speech into your ears! And you're going to give it directly to the audience. Take your time. Make it your own. This space is all yours. We start when the music stops. Over to you.

Bach stops.

Scene 5

The following speech is prompted throughout by the HYPNOTIST who speaks inaudibly into a microphone, but whose words are picked up through the FATHER's headphones.

FATHER: Ladies and gentlemen.

Dawn went to the mortuary. I refused. If anything, in those first few days, Claire had multiplied. She had become cloned! She was between lines, inside circles, hiding beneath angles. She was indentations in time, physical depressions, imperfections on surfaces. She was the spaces beneath the chairs.

Ladies and gentlemen.

Dawn was diminished. She clung to material evidence. To her, Claire was a hair left on a bar of soap, some flowers taped to a lamp post. She was the photograph hung above the piano. For me, these things were no more of Claire than of anyone else. A photograph just looked like other photographs. Whilst I had the real thing!

Nod your head if you understand.

The house began to fill with grief. After the inquest, the undertakers appeared. Dawn and Marcy discussed which of Claire's cuddlies should go into the coffin. On the day of the funeral I went for a walk. Dawn screamed at me, but I had no one to bury.

Nod your head if you understand.

I came to the roadside. I needed a hug from my girl. I looked at a tree. A tree by the road. I touched it. And from the hollows and the spaces, I scooped up the properties of Claire and changed the physical substance of the tree into that of my daughter.

Three. Two. One.

Bach plays.

The HYPNOTIST gives the following instructions to the FATHER through the ear piece:

> '*Fantastic, X. Beautiful. I'm going to come up to you and ask you if you're okay. I'll say, 'Are you okay?' When I ask you that question take your headphones out – you will not need them again – and then ask me for a drink of water. Say, "Can I have a drink of water?"*'

Bach stops.

Scene 6

HYPNOTIST: Are you okay?

The FATHER takes out his earphones.

FATHER: Could I have a drink of water?

HYPNOTIST: Of course. Of course. I'm so sorry. I'll have to go down to the bar and get you one; I'll be no more than thirty seconds, I promise. Will you be alright on your own? Say "Yes".

FATHER: Yes.

The HYPNOTIST exits the stage to get a glass of water for the FATHER. He is gone no more than thirty seconds, leaving the FATHER alone on stage with the audience.

The sound of the roadside. Thirty seconds, during which a lorry thunders past. The sound of the roadside stops.

The HYPNOTIST returns with a glass of water for the FATHER. He invites the FATHER to sit on the piano stool, and gives him a new piece of script which contains the following scene.

The HYPNOTIST rights one of the upturned chairs from the act and sits on it.

HYPNOTIST: Okay?

FATHER: Yes.

HYPNOTIST: You're doing brilliantly.

                How are you feeling about it?

FATHER: Fine.

HYPNOTIST: Not embarrassed?

FATHER: A bit.

HYPNOTIST: You should have said, I'd have stopped.

FATHER: It's okay.

HYPNOTIST:	Still nervous?
FATHER:	A bit.
HYPNOTIST:	It doesn't show.
	I thought I saw you struggling to keep a straight face earlier on.
FATHER:	Yes.
HYPNOTIST:	When was that?
	Was it around the wiping up the shit? People usually get the giggles around then.
FATHER:	No, actually.
HYPNOTIST:	When?
FATHER:	When you said Ford Focus. I used to drive a Ford Focus.
HYPNOTIST:	No way! How funny!
	What do you think's going to happen?
FATHER:	I don't know.
HYPNOTIST:	Who's your favourite character?
FATHER:	Nobody really.
HYPNOTIST:	Do you get the story?
FATHER:	About the girl?
HYPNOTIST:	I suppose so.
FATHER:	I get that she's dead. Or is that all in his mind?
HYPNOTIST:	Whose?
FATHER:	Mine. The father's.
HYPNOTIST:	No, she really is dead.
FATHER:	And you killed her?
HYPNOTIST:	Indirectly, yes.

FATHER:	I don't understand the stuff with the tree, then.
HYPNOTIST:	No.
FATHER:	I feel sorry for his wife.
HYPNOTIST:	Dawn?
FATHER:	And his other daughter. The one who's watching *The Simpsons*.
HYPNOTIST:	Marcia.
FATHER:	How old is she meant to be?
HYPNOTIST:	I don't know. Whatever you think.
FATHER:	It feels like she's about five?
HYPNOTIST:	Five's good. She's a little under-written.
FATHER:	Yes.
	Do we ever get to see her?
HYPNOTIST:	She appears as a chair.
FATHER:	Okay
HYPNOTIST:	In about ten minutes time.
FATHER:	Okay.
	Could I ask a question about my character?
HYPNOTIST:	Of course.
FATHER:	What does he do for a living?
HYPNOTIST:	I've always assumed he's a teacher.
FATHER:	Okay.
	Of art or something?
HYPNOTIST:	I always assumed Maths, or Geography.
FATHER:	Oh.
HYPNOTIST:	Is it important?

FATHER:	Not really.
HYPNOTIST:	Are you okay if we get back to it?
FATHER:	Of course.
HYPNOTIST:	You're really good, you know. And you're doing really well.
FATHER:	So are you.
	It's really well written.
HYPNOTIST:	Thanks.
	Can I ask you to go and sit back in the audience?
FATHER:	In the pub?
HYPNOTIST:	Yes.
FATHER:	But they've all gone.
HYPNOTIST:	Yes. The show was a failure; they became embarrassed and left. It's what I'm used to. Don't worry on my behalf. For the last three months, since the accident, I've been – I've lost all ability. Like I said, honouring old bookings.
FATHER:	I'm sorry.
HYPNOTIST:	I've lost my mojo! Have to think about a career change. Could be worse, I could be dead!
	God, I'm sorry. I'm so sorry.
FATHER:	It's fine. It's not really me.
HYPNOTIST:	Of course not.
FATHER:	And anyway, it hasn't happened yet.
HYPNOTIST:	What?
FATHER:	You said it's a year from now.

HYPNOTIST:	Yes! Of course.
FATHER:	So.
	If you'll excuse me.
HYPNOTIST:	Of course.
FATHER:	If we're a year in the future –
HYPNOTIST:	Yes.
FATHER:	– and the accident was three months ago
HYPNOTIST:	Go on.
FATHER:	– then, on another level, the accident's also going to happen in nine months time. Nine months from now, here, in the theatre. Is that right?
HYPNOTIST:	I suppose so.
FATHER:	This sounds stupid but –
HYPNOTIST:	Go on.
FATHER:	Is there nothing we can do to stop it happening?
HYPNOTIST:	I'm so sorry.
FATHER:	You will help me, though, won't you?
HYPNOTIST:	I don't see what else I can do –
FATHER:	Dawn says I need closure.
HYPNOTIST:	I'm not really a therapist.
FATHER:	I've thought about suicide.
HYPNOTIST:	I –
	Three. Two. One.

Scene 7

Music plays loud. The come-on-down music from the HYPNOTIST's act.

During the music, the HYPNOTIST provides the FATHER with a script and a microphone and instructs him/her directly on what to do.

The HYPNOTIST picks up another chair and places it behind the FATHER's piano stool, where the HYPNOTIST will sit, his back to the FATHER and the audience.

Music stops.

FATHER: Dawn.

               Dawn.

HYPNOTIST: Sssh.

FATHER: Dawn.

HYPNOTIST: What?

FATHER: You still crying?

HYPNOTIST: I'd just got to sleep. I was sleeping.

FATHER: It's okay.

HYPNOTIST: Andy.

FATHER: I wanted to read something to you.

HYPNOTIST: You'll wake Marcy.

FATHER   Help you to relax. It's from one of the books – the books they left – You don't have to do anything.

HYPNOTIST: I can't stand this. I was asleep, Andy.

FATHER: Listen. It's a script. It will help you.

HYPNOTIST: Please.

The FATHER will read the following speech, through the microphone.

At the same time, the HYPNOTIST will get increasingly distraught and upset, delivering Dawn's words over the FATHER's speech.

Gradually the 'hypnotic' music from the stage act starts to be heard – playing from the same place as the Bach and the roadside. This will build slowly throughout.

FATHER: **I want you to imagine that you are lying on a golden sandy beach. And as you lie under the warmth of the sun, I want you to feel all the muscles in your body are beginning to relax. All the tension is beginning to melt away.**

HYPNOTIST: I can't bear this.

FATHER: **Your heels are sinking gently into the soft, warm sand.**

HYPNOTIST: Stop this, Andy, please. What's happening?

FATHER: **Your ankles, your calves, the backs of your knees, your thighs, your buttocks, your sacrum, the small of your back, your spine sinks down, vertebrae by vertebrae, your rib cage, your shoulders, the nape of the neck, the back of the neck, your head.**

HYPNOTIST: Has it not sunk in yet? Is that what's happened? Well it had better soon, because I can't do this on my own. I can't stand this. It's three o'clock in the morning, Andy, and our beautiful daughter is lying in a fridge somewhere and you're asking me to relax my fucking knees.

FATHER: **Sinking further and further, relaxing deeper and deeper. All tension bleeding out of your body and into the golden sands. As you breathe in and out, in and out, I want you to be receptive to the thought that you're letting go of all** anxiety, fear, sadness, anger, grief or any other feeling and emotion that is holding you back.

HYPNOTIST: Don't you go mad on me, man. I need you. This is hell. If it weren't for Marcy I'd be under a car. I'd be at the bottom of a lake, off a bridge, under a train, hanging from a fucking beam. Don't you feel it? Oh god, oh god. You don't get it. Claire's gone, Andy. She's gone.

FATHER: **You're breathing now in rhythm with the waves that are gently lapping at your feet. The water is clear and sparkling. It is glinting in the dappled sunshine. As the water plays around your body you begin to make a conscious connection from your heart to the whole of creation. And as you breathe, you feel your body sinking lower and lower into the sand, at all times supported by the earth that is so rich, so abundant, so unconditional that her energies can provide you with all you're asking for.**

HYPNOTIST: You're not even listening. It's like some abstract intellectual fucking concept for you, isn't it. Claire's death. She never existed for you in the first place, did she? She was just some idea. The idea of a daughter, just as I'm the idea of a wife. Marcy's idea of a child. We don't exist for you, do we, not in flesh and blood. So you haven't lost anything, have you. She's still there, in your head, where she was in the first fucking place. Well I have. I fucking have. Help me.

FATHER: **Here begin to create the intention of collecting the subtle qualities you require to help you on your life's**

> journeys, such as balance, health, clarity,
> courage. Be aware that as the waters lap
> around you, your body sinks under and
> is redeemed of all loss, all negativity.
> And when at last the waters recede, they
> leave you feeling completely refreshed
> and totally relaxed.

The trance music stops.

> These are instructions for a mental
> exercise. Practice each day for one hour.
> Use caution in releasing yourself at the
> end of each period of exercise.

Bach plays. The HYPNOTIST instructs the FATHER.

HYPNOTIST: Fantastic, X! This music's going to play. I'm
                going to come and stand downstage. When
                the music stops I want you to give me that
                next line on your script – the line is, 'You've
                woken Marcy.' And then we're going to
                carry on with the scene.

                You are doing brilliantly.

Bach stops.

FATHER: You've woken Marcy.

HYPNOTIST: I need to clear this up. Pack the car. Could I
                have the microphone please.

The FATHER hands the HYPNOTIST the microphone.

                All this stuff is mine, the speakers – I suppose
                I should sell it. I sold that Focus.

FATHER: Do I stay here? Do I stay sitting?

HYPNOTIST: I don't know.

FATHER: You said I was doing brilliantly.

HYPNOTIST: You are.

FATHER: You said we could stop if I wasn't enjoying it.

HYPNOTIST: That was just a thing to say, to encourage
              you.

FATHER: I want to stop.

HYPNOTIST: Listen.

              She just stepped out. That's all. I went round
              to the front of the car. You could still hear the
              music from her headphones.

FATHER: She could really play.

HYPNOTIST: I'm sure she could.

FATHER: I loved to listen to her, watch her fingers.

HYPNOTIST: I have to go, Andy. Or they'll kick us out.

FATHER: And then tonight!

              I couldn't play the piano before tonight.
              Didn't know I could play.

              I was good, wasn't I?

HYPNOTIST: Stand up.

              Stand here.

The HYPNOTIST positions the FATHER in relation to the piano stool and takes away his script.

              You're cold in this rain.

HYPNOTIST: Three, two, one.

The sound of the roadside.

The HYPNOTIST is there, holding a chair on his hip, as he would a five-year-old girl.

HYPNOTIST: Are you coming home?

              Come home, it's fucking freezing.

The HYPNOTIST may feed the FATHER the following instruction: 'Don't repeat anything now. Just listen to what you say.'

> You say, 'I can't leave'.
>
> I say, 'She's not here'. You say, 'You can't see'.
>
> I say, 'Where then? Where is she?' You say, 'Here. Here'.
>
> I say, 'It's a tree, Andy. It's just a fucking tree'. You say, 'No, you're wrong'.
>
> I say, 'It's alright, Marcy. Daddy's poorly. Oh, you're frozen, you poor thing. Let's get you home.
>
> I say, 'Look, she's lost her sister. She's not going to lose her fucking father, too.
>
> I say, 'We all have to deal with this. Cope with this. We have to get on. See things for what they are.'
>
> Point at the piano stool.
>
> Say, 'Look, Dawn, look'.

FATHER: Look, Dawn, look.

HYPNOTIST: Say, 'It's not a tree anymore.'

FATHER: It's not a tree anymore.

HYPNOTIST: Say, 'You're not looking'.

FATHER: You're not looking.

HYPNOTIST: Say, 'I've changed it into Claire'.

FATHER: I've changed it into Claire.

HYPNOTIST: I say, 'Our girl is dead, love. She's dead'.

> I say, 'That is a tree, I am your wife, this is your daughter, that is a road. This is what

matters. This. This is what we have to deal with. This.'

The sound of a lorry thundering past.

The roadside noise ends.

The HYPNOTIST gets the FATHER to sit on the chair that was playing Marcia and hands him a script. The HYPNOTIST then sits on the piano stool.

HYPNOTIST: Is it how you imagined it?

FATHER: What?

HYPNOTIST: Doing this.

FATHER: The whole coming on stage thing?

HYPNOTIST: Yes, the whole thing.

FATHER: I didn't really know what to expect.

HYPNOTIST: Why did you agree?

FATHER: It sounded interesting.

HYPNOTIST: Don't you think it's a bit contrived?

FATHER: Hard to tell from here.

HYPNOTIST: Of course.

               Have you seen any of my other work?

FATHER: No.

               Also –

               Dawn says it's as though there's been two deaths. She says if I don't sort my head out soon she's taking Marcy.

               So I ought to do something.

               I think it's because I never went to the morgue.

               If I'd been able to see her for one last time. If I'd been able to say goodbye.

If I could just say goodbye.

And when I saw your name on a poster.

HYPNOTIST: You thought I could help with that?

FATHER: Say.

Say, 'I'm sorry'.

HYPNOTIST: I'm sorry.

FATHER: Say, 'I have to pack up'.

HYPNOTIST: I have to pack up.

You know there wasn't a piano.

FATHER: What?

HYPNOTIST: Earlier. There wasn't really a piano.

FATHER: Yes. I played it. I played it earlier on.

HYPNOTIST: No. That was just me playing some music and saying that there was.

FATHER: No.

I really played it.

Scene 8

Music plays, loud. Carmina Burana 'O Fortuna'.

As the music plays, the HYPNOTIST gives a series of instructions to the FATHER.

HYPNOTIST: These are the last speeches in the play. We give them directly to the audience. Take your time. Make them your own. We start when the music stops.

'O Fortuna' cuts out. Both actors read from scripts directly out to the audience. As the two actors read, the Bach begins to play, quietly.

HYPNOTIST: When I say so, you're driving.

It's dusk. The sky is purple, blue, orange, yellow, grey.

To your right, the rim of the world is blackening.

You're on your way to somewhere. You're not too tired.

You shift your weight. You shift your weight again.

You glance at the mirror. You catch sight of the upper left-hand corner of your face.

You're 51.

You're driving forward in space and time.

FATHER: When I say so, you're walking.

It's dusk.

You're on your way to somewhere. You shift your weight. You shift your weight again.

You're 12.

The air is cold. You're listening to music. You're not too tired.

You're walking forward in space and time.

HYPNOTIST: When I count to three, you're cornering. You're reaching for a cigarette.

Nod your head if you understand.

FATHER: When I count to three you're dreaming of winter and supper and Futurama. Your cheeks are flushed with the cold.

Nod your head if you understand.

HYPNOTIST: When I click my fingers, you're swerving. Your hands are gripping the steering wheel, your foot is jabbing hard on the brakes.

FATHER: When I click my fingers, you're stepping off the kerb.

HYPNOTIST: When I say sleep, a girl is there. Her eyes are wide open.

When I say sleep, she looks at you.

When I say sleep everything slows.

FATHER: When I say sleep a car is coming towards you. You're listening to music.

When I say sleep, the music stops.

HYPNOTIST: When I say sleep, she lifts her hand up.

When I say sleep, you say goodbye.

FATHER: When I say sleep, everything stops

HYPNOTIST: When I say sleep, you're free again.

FATHER: When I say sleep, you're free.

FATHER: When I say sleep, everything stops.

HYPNOTIST: Sleep.

FATHER: Sleep.

HYPNOTIST: When you open your eyes.

FATHER: When you open your eyes.

The music passes through into the First Variation, which plays forcefully through to an end.

Blackout.

The End.

ENGLAND
A PLAY FOR GALLERIES

ENGLAND – audience moving through exhibition by
Isa Genzken, Whitechapel Gallery, London, 2009

Commissioned by the Traverse Theatre, Edinburgh.

Co-produced by Culturgest, Lisbon, Warwick Arts Centre and News from Nowhere.

Premiered at the Fruitmarket Gallery, Edinburgh, 4 August 2007

Performed by Tim Crouch and Hannah Ringham

Co-directed by Karl James and a smith
Sound by Dan Jones

to Julia

'One has to have died already to be there.'

Brian O'Doherty
inside the White Cube

Act One

DABBING

A room in an art gallery (in this case say The Fruitmarket Gallery in Edinburgh) containing an exhibition of work (in this case say Alex Hartley).

Two actors as guides to the exhibition – one male and one female.

Until the guides begin to speak, the only focus to the audience is the exhibition of work that exists in the gallery.

> Thank you.
>
> Thanks very much.
>
> Thanks.
>
> Ladies and gentlemen.
>
> Thank you.
>
> If it weren't for you, I wouldn't be here.
>
> You saved my life!
>
>
> Welcome to the Fruitmarket Gallery here in Edinburgh.
>
> World class contemporary art at the heart of the city.
>
>
> (We'll be here for around 30 minutes and then we'll go to another room.
>
> Where we can sit down.)

As the name suggests, the building we are in was built as a fruit and vegetable market in 1938.

The Scottish Arts Council converted the market into a visual arts space in 1974.

This is the space we're in now.

Look.

It's beautiful.

Thank you Scottish Arts Council. If it weren't for you, we wouldn't be here.

You saved our lives!!

The Fruitmarket doesn't only exhibit work by Scottish artists, but also work by artists from all around the world – Chinese, Danish, German, Australian, Japanese, Italian, French, Russian, Canadian, Israeli, Icelandic, Dutch, Portuguese.

And, of course, American.

This current exhibition is of work by an artist called Alex Hartley.

Alex is English.

I hope you will make time while you're in Edinburgh to get to know Alex's work.

Please don't touch anything.

I'm also English.

My boyfriend is American.

But he's actually Dutch.

No one in America is really American!

My boyfriend has three passports.

He calls me kiddo.

'Hey kiddo'!

Hoe doet u, kiddo?

Ik ben zeer goed, dank u!

My boyfriend can speak 4 different languages. He's a citizen of the world!

I have no languages.

Everyone speaks English!

A sound starts. There is an underscoring from now to the end of Act One – drifting in and out, building towards the end.

We live in London.

We love London!

We love London!

It's such a great place to live.

The city is dynamic and progressive. But it's so expensive. I couldn't afford to live here if it wasn't for my boyfriend.

My boyfriend buys and sells art for other people. He tells them what to buy – what's up and what's down. He travels the world.

He's never been to The Fruitmarket Gallery.
He'd love it if he came here.

He'd think it was fantastic. He'd love all
these clean lines.

My boyfriend and I have been together for
8 years.

Which is pretty fantastic, too!

He saved my life.

If it weren't for him, I wouldn't be here.

Look!

Look!

Here you can see me in the night.

Here you can see me leaning.

Here you can see me in the early morning.

Look. I've been sleeping on the sofa.

Look.

Look!

This is the view out there.

Look at the sun from the windows.

Look how the reflections from the buildings
around us convey a sense of depth.

Look! My skin is damp with sweat.

Look!

I've left a stain on the fabric of the sofa!

My boyfriend's about to go to an art fair in Munich. He says it's like a yard sale. He's looking for Gothic woodprints. He has a client in Pennsylvania who is building a Bavarian Schloss.

A castle outside Pittsburgh!

Look.

Look!

Here he is giving me a glass of water.

Here he is saying to me that I should have woken him.

'Take a day off!' he's saying.

His skin is smooth.

He's going to Munich!

Munich is a thousand miles away.

I'm curled up on the sofa.

Look.

I'm so small.

Something's wrong.

Something's wrong with me.

The tone of the sound changes.

This is where we live, my boyfriend and me.

We live in Southwark. / Here.

We live in a converted jam factory / in Southwark.

Here, in Southwark. In / London.

In England.

We have a duplex.

We have white walls.

It's like heaven here!

Here.

Here.

We don't have much here, but what we have is pretty amazing.

We have a Marcus Taylor on the wall. He's a favourite of ours. His colours are amazing.

My boyfriend believes that art shouldn't just be in galleries. / It belongs in people's everyday lives.

Art is for all!

He's not a collector. He just gets what he likes.

We have a Gregory Crewdson and a small Gary Hume.

We have a Marc Quinn and a Tacita Dean.

In the other room, seriously, we have a small Willem de Kooning. / Seriously.

Seriously. It's not a joke.

Nobody believes us when we say it's the real thing.

They think it's a fake, but it's not!

We have a certificate.

Some people think that I did it!

Do I look like an artist?

We regulate the temperature and humidity.

Look.

de Kooning is one of the most famous American painters in the world.

One of the most famous painters in the world!

He is an abstract expressionist.

He was born in Rotterdam in 1904 but he came to America when he was 22.

He was an immigrant.

He died in 1997. He had Alzheimers. Some people say he got it from all the lead in the paint he used.

Art is deadly!

My boyfriend bought the painting at auction in 1995 – from a Swiss collector.

With a little bit of help from his father.

It's always good to buy art just before the artist dies, because after they die it goes up in value.

When they're dead, we know for sure they won't be able to paint any more!

Thank god!

The painting is unfinished, from a series of two studies for a canvas he did in 1952. My boyfriend paid an arm and a leg for it, but he loves de Kooning. My boyfriend's father is from Rotterdam, too, so that's why. Friends say we should put it in safe storage. But it's insured for a million pounds, which is more than twice what he paid for it at auction in 1995 from a Swiss collector.

It's worth more than this duplex!

And it's not even finished!!

Can you imagine?

I get scared to touch it.

Don't touch it, kid!

Raak het niet, kid!

Het is heel wat geld waard!

My boyfriend understands the market.

My boyfriend says that he can still smell the jam.

In the corners!

If you look at the lintel above the door, you can see the imprint of the Architect – the set square, the compass and the pyramid.

There used to be a wall here.

We don't make jam!

I've had a bad / night again.

This is leasehold.

Silence.

There are postcards / in the bookshop.

I can't concentrate.

The sound resumes.

My boyfriend's back from Munich now. He was outbid for a Durer by a dealer from Osaka.

He's angry that he missed it.

He's grumpy with me.

Fucking Japs, he says!

He hates / it when I'm ill.

He wants us to make love, but I don't feel well enough.

My skin / is sore.

Not now.

I'm never ill!

Look.

I'm sorry.

He's pretending that it doesn't matter, but I know that it does.

Look.

Where's my / strength gone?

Where's my?

Where?

Can't lift / my feet.

Can't get to the bathroom in the night.

Please don't get the wrong idea about my boyfriend, though. I'm embarrassed that you should see him like this. / He's a really good guy.

He believes in art!

We have a Marc Quinn!

I feel inadequate next to him.

Look.

I'm useless. What's happening to me? Something's wrong with me! I'm worried that he will become distant towards me.

Look.

I love him so much. I lie awake and listen to my boyfriend breathing. I listen to the horses galloping in my chest. I feel all alone in the world. I wonder what it would be like to be dead.

I hate it when my boyfriend doesn't get what he wants. I wonder if everything stops. I wonder if there's an afterlife. There must be. All this beauty can't just stop, can it!

All these clean lines!

Here.

Here in The Fruitmarket Gallery.

My boyfriend's father is Presbyterian. His company donates 10% of its profits to the church.

He sponsored a sculpture park for a cancer ward in Atlanta in Georgia.

My boyfriend's father did well in America.

He puts back what he gets out!

He won't come here, / though.

Look at the photographs.

Look at the floor! When we bought this place it was photographs of wood made to look like real wood! We replaced it with real wood!

Look.

My boyfriend has been to Korea.

He's been / to Lahore.

To Beijing.

To Madrid.

To Venice.

He's buying and selling!

Art is universal.

Here you can see my boyfriend talking
on the phone. He's talking to a colleague
in Zurich. I don't understand a word he's
saying.

He's my lover and I don't understand what
he's saying to his colleague in Zurich!

I don't have any languages.

His eyes are red from traveling. I don't think
it's too late here. Maybe about 9. Or 9.30
maybe. Or later. Or earlier. Look at the light
on the bookshelf. He brought it back from
Japan.

Look at the angles / and the parallel lines.

Look at the light.

Look.

My boyfriend is so strong. When he holds
me I feel his strength come into me.

My boyfriend is wearing a new belt.

He's traveling.

Air travel is so cheap!

My boyfriend laughs with his hands inside
his pockets.

If you look, I'm going to the doctors. It's a
beautiful day in Southwark in London. From
where we're standing, we can see the Tower
of London, Tower Bridge, the new County
Hall, the Gherkin.

Note also Guy's Hospital, the Battleship HMS Belfast, the Globe Theatre and the tower of Tate Modern. So much to see it turns my head.

I used to like it when everything moved so quickly, but now I get dizzy.

My ankles are swollen. / Look.

I'm tired.

This isn't / my skin!

This isn't me.

This isn't me.

Our apartment is really near here! Near the water. Southwark has really seen a regeneration in recent years. / Property is so expensive.

It can't stay like that forever.

In 2006, a whale was spotted as far upstream as Chelsea!

A whale in central London! As my boyfriend would say, Wie dat zou geloven?!

Wie dat zou geloven?!

This is my doctor's surgery. / It's near London Bridge.

It's bright and airy.

On the walls are prints by Raoul Dufy, David Hockney and Seurat.

A translation service is available.

Look.

Look.

The patients like to look at the paintings. It helps them feel better about their illnesses.

Near my doctor's surgery is a place called Vinopolis – which has wine from all over the world. People can go on guided tours through the wine cellars under a viaduct built in 1866. My boyfriend and I did that. We love wine. We love Vinopolis. Vinopolis started in 1999. 1999 is when me and my boyfriend got together.

On New Year's Eve!

The New Millenium.

Happy New Year!

Sit up here.

Breathe in.

Listen.

Breathe in.

Listen.

Listen again.

Look.

I'm a good patient.

This is cashmere!

Dr Kumar is sympathetic.

He asks me about my family.

He asks me about / my next of kin.

My boyfriend is my next of kin.

This is Southwark cathedral. I like to come
here when I've been to the doctors. Here or
to the Tate Modern gallery, which is only
about just a stone's throw from here. From /
Southwark Cathedral.

Here.

Doctor Kumar is my GP. He's great. If
it wasn't for him I wouldn't be here. But
sometimes I can't understand what he's
saying. It's frustrating. Especially if you are a
doctor and need to say things clearly about
how people are and how / people are feeling.

There's no room for ambiguity in the
medical profession!

It's not an art form!

I have a stabbing pain!

I have a shooting pain!

I have a burning pain!

I think Southwark Cathedral is my favourite
cathedral.

I used to bring my boyfriend here.

It's a good place for me to sit and think about things.

Here in Southwark Cathedral.

I enjoy the peace. I enjoy the clean lines and the feel and look of the stone.

Everyone talks so quietly.

It's beautiful.

It's like heaven.

Look.

We're standing now in the Nave

Notice the central boss, in the form of a shield supported by angels. On this shield you can see the symbols of our Lord's suffering, / the nails, the crown of thorns, the scourge and the cross.

I feel like I'm sliding around. / I feel swollen up. I feel beached.

These are the works of an artist on the wall and in the cathedral.

This is art.

Look at me!

Look.

Here comes my boyfriend again. He's on the way to Istanbul, with a shopping list. He knows so much. He's learning Chinese.

I am in such pain here! It comes over me.
Look.

Look at the colours in the corners of the
eyes!

Look at my / fingernails!

The half moons!

My boyfriend sits by me. He feels for me so
much that he doesn't want to leave me. But
someone's got to support how we live. Look.

I'm bringing out my boyfriend's religious
side. He used to be agnostic.

He never used to pray. And now he prays for
me!

I must be in trouble!

All this is art.

All this is art.

This is how we look.

Look.

We're a couple.

The sound builds in intensity.

When I'm with my boyfriend I think that anything is possible.

I feel indestructible!

I wish that I wasn't so ill so that we could have sex.

We used to have / really good sex.

I don't feel erotic.

He knows so much about art, which is why he would love it here, in the Fruitmarket Gallery in Edinburgh. I don't know anything, really. I look at these things and I don't really understand them. I like them, but my boyfriend would understand them. He would interpret them for me.

He says that good art is art that sells.

He's taught me the difference between looking and seeing!

This is Guy's Hospital in London.

Look.

Look.

Look at the atrium.

Look at the clean lines.

I'm on the art trail. It connects the works of art in the hospital, with information about the artists and the therapeutic benefits of art in health.

This work is called African Woman With Child.

It's beautiful.

Don't / touch it!

Even clean hands leave marks and damage surfaces!

My boyfriend would love it here in Guy's Hospital. He would love the quiet and the spirit of the hospital. He would recognise the importance of art in recuperation and contemplation.

Art can make you feel better about going to die.

It can make you live longer!

Can you imagine?

Thanks, art!

If it weren't for you we wouldn't be here.

You saved our lives!

Doctor Frempong is a great man. He's always optimistic! / Look at what he did for me!

He took a photograph of / my heart!

My arteries!

He saved my life. If it weren't for him, I wouldn't be here. Doctor Frempong comes from Ghana. His family still live in Ghana.

Doctor Frempong tells me to smile with my heart!

I need this rail to keep my balance!

Guy's Hospital was founded in 1719.

17 / 24.

1721.

Guy's Hospital was / founded.

This is in August.

This is August.

Atrial Fibrillation is when the atria and the ventricles of the heart beat at a different rate. This causes an abnormal rhythm of the heart, an arrhythmia, leading to palpitations, weakness, shortness of breath and dizziness.

I've been on the sofa again.

These bricks are original!

If you look closely you can see the chest heave and gallop.

I'm by the window.

There's no whale in the river today!

My boyfriend is going to Moscow.

This is the bathroom. /

I've been throwing up!

I'm in a car!

Look at the juxtaposition!

We're making plans.

Look / at the tones.

Any questions?

Gifts and books are in / the gift shop.

The cafe is closed.

Because of this.

My boyfriend and I are discussing
arrangements.

Look.

I will want to be buried.

I will decide on which music to / be played.

Which poem is to be read.

My boyfriend doesn't want to talk about it.
He doesn't believe it will happen.

He's death-defying!

I'm so tired.

I can't breathe.

Look how small / I have become!

I'm disappearing!

Look at the shallowness of my breathing.

Look at the pulse at the side of my head.

Look at the weakness.

Listen to the helicopter blades.

Everything is an effort.

Look!

My skin is grey!

My boyfriend is amazing. He makes me feel safe.

Alex Hartley is a leading artist. As well as the Fruit Market here in Edinburgh and the Victoria Miro gallery in London, he has exhibited at the Louisiana Museum of Modern Art in Denmark; the Museum of Contemporary Art in Sarajevo; the Distrito Cuatro in Madrid; the Kunstlerhaus in Dortmund and the National Museum of Art in Osaka, Japan.

In 2004 Alex claimed sovereignty of a new Arctic island in the region of Svalbard in Norway. Revealed by the melting of the Arctic ice, the chunk of rock measures the size of a football pitch.

Alex has given it the name Nymark, which means new world in Norweigan.

As the ice melts, he says, new landscapes emerge.

The symptoms of Hypertrophic Cardiomyopathy can develop very suddenly. Every possible avenue of treatment is explored before the issue of transplant is addressed.

Here I am at a Hospital near Cambridge. My boyfriend drove me here.

This is in the countryside.

My boyfriend is shouting.

We are in a car park.

I am shaking.

Look.

The colours are bright.

It's a beautiful day.

Look.

The leaves are leaving the branches.

Everything is spinning away from me.

It's beautiful.

This is in London or in Southwark.

My boyfriend is on the phone to his father. His father runs a company in Atlanta. My boyfriend's father's company in Atlanta makes components in Atlanta Georgia.

My boyfriend's father is talking to his son about what is to be done. / They talk in English and in Dutch.

I don't understand them.

When my boyfriend is on the phone to his father he looks so cute. / He calls him sir. Americans are so respectful.

My boyfriend says that this shouldn't be happening to us! That we should have gone private. That we're going to fight this. Here he is telling me that he loves me.

Look.

Look.

This is waiting.

Silence.

We're waiting.

Sound resumes.

My cardiologist is called Mrs Raad. She is from the Lebanon. If it weren't for her, / I wouldn't be here.

She saved my life.

Mrs Raad reminds us that the waiting list is horizontal.

She reminds us to pack a bag.

She reminds us to be ready.

She reminds us to keep the pager on for when a new heart is coming.

We're waiting.

Artwork can bring many therapeutic benefits to patients, visitors and staff within a hospital environment.

My boyfriend's father runs a company in Atlanta.

My boyfriend's father recommends a friend of a friend who might be able to help. He says that America has a lot of friends. / He is just like his son.

He's so positive.

My boyfriend is standing on our balcony with the phone. The phone is tucked under his chin. He is watching the river / and talking to a man 4000 miles away.

I am in bed with my / oxygen.

My boyfriend and my boyfriend's father pray for me down the telephone lines, through the microwaves.

Look.

I can't concentrate.

Look!

My skin is shedding.

I'm dying.

I'm dying.

I am led to understand by the people we have talked / to that this is it.

I understand this.

This is.

Everything is packing up! Look.

Look!

It's / so beautiful.

It's so frightening.

At night.

Here you can see me in the early morning.

Whatever.

Whatever.

Is.

Is this.

This.

Something.

Happening.

Look at the muscles in the heart. Look at them thickening. Look at how the pumping chamber gets smaller and keeps the heart muscle from relaxing properly between contractions. Look how the chambers of the heart stiffen as the muscle thickens.

It's happening to me here.

This is the picture.

Look!

Look!

I'm ready.

I'm ready even.

Ready.

What's / one less?

Really.

What's one less?

I will die either from sudden collapse, collapse without warning due to a collapse from sudden and severe arrhythmia. Or my heart will just fail in its job of pumping oxygenated blood around my body and I will pass into an unconsciousness and I will die.

I hope it will be sudden. Out in a blaze of glory.

Come on.

This way / please.

Follow me.

This is us waiting.

My boyfriend has spilt his wine.

My boyfriend is crying.

My boyfriend is / angry.

Is standing.

Is tensing.

Is.

My boyfriend is.

Look at the angles.

He says I have become defeatist.

That is defeatist talk.

I am being strong for him.

This is in Edinburgh.

It's maybe 8.20. Or 8.30.

Look at the light from the window.

The gallery will be closing.

I don't believe the phone will ring.

My beeper will not beep.

I don't know what will happen. Just
nothingness, I suppose. There was me and /
then there was not me.

There was me and then there was not me.

In Munich.

In Madrid.

In Osaka.

In Oslo.

In Rotterdam.

In Berlin.

In Kabul.

In Edinburgh.

It's good that my boyfriend can't hear me
talking like this.

He believes that anything is possible.

He believes in art.

If I died, I think my boyfriend would move back to the States.

People don't stay in foreign countries forever. At some point they get a call deep inside them to go back to their homeland. The place they understand.

Their heartland.

My heartland is here.

We are all at the / end of our

At the end of / our

End of

Our / patience.

My boyfriend has lost his / patience, too.

At the end of our patience with / everything.

He's losing everything.

It is not civilized.

To be like this.

To sit like this.

To grip like this.

To shake like this.

I was not led to believe that it would / be like this.

My boyfriend likes to be in control, but / he can't be.

This is intolerable.

He's having an outburst.

He says this wouldn't happen in the United States of America.

I'm / sorry.

I'm so sorry.

You shouldn't / have to see this.

I've really failed, haven't I? I've failed.

I'm so / so sorry.

I really really fucked up everything.

Everything.

I do not want / to be here.

This is not the right place to be.

Nowhere is the / right place to be.

There is no place to accommodate how I am and how I feel.

I don't like you to see my boyfriend like this. He's such a great guy. He's just at the end of his tether, to see his loved one like this.

He said he'd do / anything for me.

He'd do anything for me.

Anything.

Any.

Any.

Any questions?

I think I DO want to die.

The sound nearly reaches a climax.

The sound stops abruptly.

The sound of Rooks and bird song.

We're standing in the grounds of a stately home in the Royal County of Berkshire.

Look.

It's beautiful. A real English autumn afternoon.

Look.

I'm not too good in this cold air.

I'm not standing. I'm in a wheel chair! My boyfriend is behind me!

My oxygen is in a cradle at the back of my chair.

This building was designed in 1768 for the Earl of Renfrewshire. It's beautiful.

The house that you see today is a result of changes made in 1830 when the west wing was gutted by fire. In the rebuild, the architect transformed the main facade in the Indian style – adding the domes and minarets that give the house its distinctive appearance today.

The building has been a private residence, a
hotel and a conference centre. In 2004 it was
purchased by an international consortium.

Architecture is like a living organism,
adapting to the culture of its time. Nobody
wants to live in a museum.

We're here to see a leading heart surgeon
who has agreed to see what he can do for
me. It helps to have a rich boyfriend.

On the walls of the clinic are a genuine
Bridget Riley, a Damien Hirst spin painting
and a photograph by Sam Taylor-Wood.
Don't touch them.

It's so beautiful.

It's so beautiful.

It's like being in a church. Or in a gallery.
Everyone talks so quietly. Everything is so
clean.

The end of the world.

*A deafening sound of splitting and destruction that leads the audience
out of the first gallery space and into the second.*

Act Two

WRINGING

A different room in the gallery.

Seats for the audience.

The wife is us, the audience. When the audience enter the space, it is her entering the space. The Interpreter interprets her 'words' and translates what is said to her.

Unless indicated, all text is delivered directly out to individual members of the audience.

ENGLISH: Thank you.

INTERPRETER: Thank you.

ENGLISH: Thank you!
                       If it weren't for you I wouldn't be here!

INTERPRETER: If it weren't for you I wouldn't be here.

ENGLISH: You saved my life!!

INTERPRETER: You saved my life.

ENGLISH: Look!

INTERPRETER: Look.

                       Silence.

ENGLISH: Never thought I'd be here. Never thought I'd
                       see this or meet you or anything, really! It's
                       amazing!! People at home think I'm crazy
                       but I've been imagining this. Since I was ill.

You know? Imagining coming here. Meeting you. Thanking you face to face.

I am so grateful to you. And honoured to meet you.

It is an honour to meet you!

INTERPRETER: I never thought I'd meet you.

ENGLISH: I've brought something for you. A gift to say thank you. Thank you to you!

From me. For me! For my life! For what you did for me!

INTERPRETER: It's an honour to meet you. I have a gift to thank you.

Silence.

ENGLISH: Would she like some refreshments ask her? Would she like some tea? Or a Coke?

There's a machine out in the corridor. Or we could phone room service.

I could easily and there's ice. There's ice in the corridor.

Are they allowed Coke?

I can't thank her enough, tell her.

INTERPRETER: Would you like something to drink?

I didn't want to see you. I didn't want anything to do with you. When I thought about you I felt sick. But then I spoke to my brother and he told me it would be the best thing. It would help me to move, to move forward.

I didn't think I could look at you.

My brother lives in Australia. In Sydney. I haven't seen my brother.

This hasn't been an easy time for me. My family aren't together.

My cousin won't see you. He'll wait in the lobby until we've finished and then he'll take me back. I can't travel on my own.

Why has this happened to my family?

Why has this happened?

I want to know why this has happened to me.

I want to know if you have an answer.

ENGLISH: I understand.

INTERPRETER: I understand.

ENGLISH: I am so sorry for your loss.

INTERPRETER: I'm sorry for your loss.

ENGLISH: It must have been unbearable.

I was ill. In my country, tell her.

INTERPRETER: I was ill.

ENGLISH: Very ill. I was going to die. You wouldn't recognise me! The doctors couldn't help me.

Tell her.

INTERPRETER: I was going to die.

ENGLISH: Look, I am well again. Look. It's a miracle!

INTERPRETER: I am well now.

ENGLISH: I take a lot of pills! But look! So far so good. The doctors say I'm doing very well, tell her! Look!

                      I'm jogging now. Run a marathon!

INTERPRETER: I am well now.

ENGLISH: I understand if it is difficult for her.

                      It was difficult to find you! To find you!

                      Does she understand anything?

INTERPRETER: You were difficult to find.

ENGLISH: I hope this place is alright for her – It was / recommended by the Embassy –

INTERPRETER: It's fine.

ENGLISH: I didn't know where we should meet, you know, somewhere neutral.

INTERPRETER: It's not an issue. / This is fine.

ENGLISH: It's clean at any rate. Same all over the world!

                      Horrible lighting!

Silence.

                      Your husband – Hassam.

INTERPRETER: Your husband, Hassam.

ENGLISH: Hassam. Does she understand anything? Your husband. Hassam. What was he like?

INTERPRETER: What was your husband like?

ENGLISH: What did he like? What did he do?

INTERPRETER: He was a good man. He loved me. He loved
                his country. He loved this world. He was 26.
                He was just a good man.

INTERPRETER: Of course. I'm sorry.

                Is she – ?

                I wanted to ask a question about her
                husband.

                Tell her.

INTERPRETER: I want to ask a question about Hassam.

ENGLISH: I wanted to ask – Did he – ? This is stupid,
                tell her.

                Since the operation, I've been having weird
                dreams – with snakes and elephants and
                monkeys, you know. I thought maybe,
                because of the – Did your husband, ask her,
                did Hassam – did he work with animals?
                Only I thought – You know you hear of
                people –

INTERPRETER: Did Hassam work with animals?

                He was going to college. He wanted to
                study to be an engineer. He wanted to go to
                university. He was a computer programmer.
                He had sponsorship to go to college. To be
                an engineer.

ENGLISH: Good. Good. Great!

                We were – I was told very little. It's very
                good to meet her, you.

                I'm so sorry.

                I have a tissue if –

                Look. If this isn't convenient –

INTERPRETER: Are you okay?

ENGLISH: Yes, 'okay'?

INTERPRETER: One moment please.

ENGLISH: Of course.

Silence.

                We could go outside?

INTERPRETER: It's fine.

ENGLISH: Must be weird for her, seeing me.

Silence.

                It's cold. You don't really associate this part
                of the world with cold.

INTERPRETER: This is winter.

ENGLISH: Of course.

Silence.

                This isn't what I expected, though. This
                traffic.

                Could be anywhere.

                My car's at four.

                Where are you from?

INTERPRETER: Manchester.

ENGLISH: Right.

Cold in Manchester!

When do you go back?

INTERPRETER: I live here.

ENGLISH: Here! Bloody hell! Good on you!

What a place.

I don't think I could live here.

Hard to see how they're feeling with just the eyes.

Meant to be a celebration.

Okay?

INTERPRETER: Do you want to continue?

She asks have you children?

ENGLISH: No.

INTERPRETER: I have a child. Until you have a child you will not know what love you have inside you. Until you know god, you will not know what love you have inside you.

ENGLISH: I understand love, and I respect her love.

INTERPRETER: You have love inside you now. Inside here. Inside. Inside Hassam's heart. Inside you. Inside God. God inside you. Inside everyone. Inside Hassam. Inside you.

ENGLISH: Thank you.

Thank you!

I will do what I can to honour that!

Does she – do you have a photograph. A photograph. Of Hassam?

INTERPRETER: Do you have a photograph?

Yes, / I have a photograph.

ENGLISH: Yes! Good. I'd be honoured to see it.

INTERPRETER: It is in my bag. With my cousin. / In the lobby.

ENGLISH: Don't worry about it. I just thought it would be / good to see a picture.

INTERPRETER: In my bag.

ENGLISH: No, no. I was just being – It's not important. / We could phone down for it. Get your cousin –

INTERPRETER: I want to show you. I want you to see him. I want you to see his face. I want you to understand what has been done.

ENGLISH: Of course.

The wife 'exits'.

Silence.

The two actors face each other.

ENGLISH: She got plenty of money, you know.

Silence.

It's been a bit of a year as you can imagine.

Coming so close to death!

You stop making plans, you know! Getting strong again, though. Not easy getting used to the idea, you know. Someone else inside you! From here! Not easy for people. Impossible for some to reconcile – You know. Damaged goods! Imperfect! No longer me. Not me anymore. Can't accept it.

But look.

Look! I feel fine! You wouldn't know, would you?

Without any movement, the two actors swap roles.

Would you? From the outside.

This is meant to be a celebration. My way of saying thank you.

Closing a chapter.

Wish I had a couple of phrases to say to her.

It's my life, though.

I mean I got my life back.

Wasn't cheap!

The wife 're-enters'.

INTERPRETER: He was 21 when the photo was taken.

ENGLISH: 21. He was very handsome.

INTERPRETER: He was handsome.

ENGLISH: I will frame it.

INTERPRETER: I will frame it.

ENGLISH: Put it in a frame – like this! Put it on my wall! On my wall!

INTERPRETER: I will put it on my wall.

ENGLISH: I will never forget your husband! Hassam.

                He is inside me. I will never forget that!

INTERPRETER: I will never forget Hassam.

Silence.

ENGLISH: Should have brought a photograph of
                myself!

                Please, tell her. If she ever wants to come
                to London. I will write to her. Send her
                photographs.

                If she needs anything. Anything.

                Tell her.

Silence.

                We heard that Hassam was in an accident.
                An accident.

INTERPRETER: Hassam was in an accident.

                No. / That's not correct.

ENGLISH: I'm so sorry. Tell her that I am sure they did
                everything they could for him.

INTERPRETER: My husband's death was not an accident.

ENGLISH: It is tragic to have a life / taken away so
                suddenly.

INTERPRETER: No.

ENGLISH: I have a gift for her. A gift. Tell her. Look.
                I brought it from England. It will change
                your life! People think I am crazy but it's
                important. You gave me my life! Hassam!

Silence.

INTERPRETER: My husband was wounded in the head and they took him to the nearest hospital – a private hospital, the Seventh Day Adventist. It's an expensive hospital. Just near here.

ENGLISH: Okay.

INTERPRETER: They told me he was very ill, that he might die. His family prayed for him – his cousin came from Berlin, another came from Paris and from Afghanistan. He was too ill to move. I went to see him. My father came with me. My husband's eyes were open a little.

His brain had been damaged. They would have to wait, if it would get better. The brain can make itself better.

ENGLISH: Right.

INTERPRETER: The hospital was very expensive. His cousin tried to raise money to keep him there. We had nothing. It was very difficult. And then a phone call from a surgeon at another clinic. A private clinic. In another city. He had been told about my husband. I thought he was offering to help him. To save his life.

I was told that someone had offered to fly my husband to this other clinic. In a helicopter. The doctors told me there was a good chance Hassam would recover so I was happy to let him go. But then I was visited by an agent from the clinic in the other city. He told me that my husband was brain dead, and that there was a client of the clinic who was prepared to pay me money if I would permit his organs to be used.

Silence.

ENGLISH: I came to give her a gift, a present, tell her.

INTERPRETER: I wanted to see you. I wanted to ask you.

Why has this has happened? Why was my husband killed? / I want to know what he had done wrong. Please tell me.

ENGLISH: Your husband wasn't killed. He was dying. He would have died. Like me! There was nothing anyone could do for him. It was for the best.

INTERPRETER: Your husband was not killed.

Yes yes.

I was told that he would live.

ENGLISH: It's difficult. The doctors can't always know. Even in my country!

INTERPRETER: A mistake.

No no no.

She's very upset. She says her husband was murdered. Everyone says he was murdered. There is great anger in his family.

ENGLISH: She doesn't understand. Tell her. Tell her. She doesn't know what I'm saying. Say what I'm saying.

INTERPRETER: You can stop this if you want.

The agent offered me 300,000 if I would give permission for my husband's heart to be taken. I couldn't believe that my husband was dead. I was told he would recover. His eyes were open. I forbade the operation. The agent told me that my husband could save a life. He said that to save the life of one is to

save the whole of mankind. He offered me
half a million for my husband's heart. I was
confused. I had nothing. My father was ill.
My husband wasn't dead. I signed a paper.
There was an American.

ENGLISH: Her husband was not killed. He wasn't
             murdered.

             I came to thank her.

             Tell her.

INTERPRETER: She understands that.

             I want to know where my husband is. I want
             to wash him, to prepare him. It is a year now.

The following speeches are played over each other.

INTERPRETER: In my country the dead body must be looked
             after. He is not a martyr. He is not. I have
             to have his body. I cannot live not knowing
             where my husband is. There is no place for
             my grief. It is unbearable. Intolerable. No
             wife should have to live with what I have
             had to live with. I am young. I have nothing.
             I received no money – a little for phone calls.
             The money went to the agent, I think. I am
             a woman alone. I have nothing. My father is
             ill. I have nothing.

ENGLISH: They said her husband was dead – not
             dead – that he was being kept alive – just
             for me. They said nothing else. They said
             nothing about moving him from anywhere.
             They said all the paperwork was correct.
             We paid a lot of money. For the transport
             and the operation. My friend dealt with it,
             really. I just saw the airport and the inside
             of the hospital, that's all. And when I was
             strong enough, they flew me back to London

for recuperation. Privately. I didn't know. I didn't know. I am still weak. I came here for her, tell her, for her.

Overlap ends.

She got money, tell her. She signed.

Fucking tell her that.

What did she say?

INTERPRETER: She says that death is god-given.

ENGLISH: I came to make a reconciliation. I came to meet – to understand what's inside me. To learn. I didn't ask to have your husband inside me. I had no say in it. I was dying and now I'm alive.

Surely that's a good thing. Life is better than death. Look. Instead of both of us being dead, one of us is alive.

I'm alive! Look!

If it had been the other way round it would have been fine. If there was no alternative.

INTERPRETER: Look. I'm alive. I was going to die but now I'm alive.

ENGLISH: Tell her to stop it.

Nobody killed your husband.

INTERPRETER: We should stop this.

ENGLISH: How am I meant to have a proper conversation when I can't even see her face.

Silence.

INTERPRETER: I never saw my husband again. When they moved him. Never again.

Silence.

She's saying that it wasn't an accident. Last year, there were – Her husband was injured in an explosion.

An explosion outside the Marriott. It killed an American official.

ENGLISH: How many dollars is half a million?

INTERPRETER: 8000.

ENGLISH: And what's the average wage here?

I have a present, a gift, to thank you, to say thank you. To help you.

I brought it from England.

INTERPRETER: I have a gift for you.

ENGLISH: It's a work of art.

INTERPRETER: A work of art.

ENGLISH: It's worth a lot of money.

It's beautiful.

You can do what you like with it. Sell it or keep it. It's yours. A lot of money. For food, or clothes, or water. For your village. For whatever you want.

A lot of money.

Does she understand? I want her to have it. I didn't have to come here. Nobody made me. This is my gift. My thank you.

            For my life.

INTERPRETER: A work of art from England.

ENGLISH: It's yours.

            Look.

INTERPRETER: She asks if she can listen to you. If she can listen at your chest.

ENGLISH: Of course.

            Here.

Silence.

INTERPRETER: She says that she recognises her husband. She can hear her husband.

            He is inside you.

ENGLISH: That's good, is it?

INTERPRETER: She says she wishes you were dead so that her husband were alive.

ENGLISH: I'm sorry.

Silence.

INTERPRETER: She asks if she can hold you.

ENGLISH: What?

INTERPRETER: Touch you. She asks if she can touch you.

Silence.

ENGLISH: What's she saying?

            What?

What's she saying?

What did she say?

What did she say?

Sound from the other space. Plays and fades.

The End.

THE AUTHOR

The Author – Royal Court Theatre, 2009

© *Stephen Cummiskey*

Commissioned by the Royal Court Theatre

Premiered at the Jerwood Theatre Upstairs, Royal Court
Theatre, London, 23 September 2009

Performed by Tim Crouch, Adrian Howells, Vic Llewellyn,
Esther Smith

Co-directed by Karl James and a smith
Lighting design by Matt Drury
Sound by Ben and Max Ringham

In a subsequent tour, the part originated by Adrian Howells
was taken by Chris Goode.

Dedicated to the memory of John Ringham, actor.

The Author is set in the Jerwood Theatre Upstairs at the Royal Court Theatre – even when it's performed elsewhere.

This is a play that happens inside its audience. As the audience enter the space, they encounter two banks of seating, facing each other, comfortably spaced apart but with no 'stage' in between. This must not be a confrontational configuration. The request the play makes is for us to be okay about ourselves, to gently see ourselves and ourselves seeing. There should be plenty of warm, open space in the play. The audience should be beautifully lit and cared for. When the audience is asked questions, these are direct questions that the audience are more than welcome to answer – but under no pressure to do so.

The actors are unspectacularly seated throughout the audience. The sometimes thwarted desire for sections of the audience to see certain actors is a dynamic of 'wanting to see' that is presented by the narrative. It is hoped that the audience will eventually feel encouraged to dispose of the need to look at whoever is speaking and enjoy their own company.

The names of the characters in this text are the names of the actors playing them for the Royal Court premiere. If the actors change, then the character names change accordingly, with the exception of the author, whose character's name should always be Tim Crouch.

Music is present in the play as a release valve. It brings us into the here and now and helps the audience to feel good about being together. It is a treat! It can play for a long time without anything happening.

An audience facing an audience in two banks of seats.

No stage area in between.

An easy, playful presence.

No sense and every sense of a play beginning.

Blank underscoring (_____) represents the names of any number of audience members that ADRIAN has effortlessly and gracefully elicited and learned. We should get to know quite a few names over the course of the play.

There is freedom in ADRIAN's speech to improvise if needed.

Space.

ADRIAN: I love this. This is great, isn't this great? I love this! This! All this! When I came in – When I came in and saw this, just this, and I thought, Oh Wow! Didn't you? Did you? Maybe you didn't. Maybe you thought Oh Jesus! Did you? Oh Jesus Christ, maybe!

Space.

This is such a versatile space. Isn't it versatile? It's amazing what they can do. They can do anything. Can't they?

Space.

I'm Adrian. I'm Adrian and you are? Hello! What's your name? Do you love this, _____? Our knees touching! Don't you? Who'll you be next to. I'm next to you! What's your name? That's beautiful. You're beautiful! Isn't _____ beautiful? Everyone?

I'll shut up. I'll stop.

Someone else go!

Space.

165

Is everyone all right?

Are you?

Space.

What are we supposed to do, I wonder? Do you know?

Sounds good, doesn't it?

Does it?

I have some cuttings in my bag. I have a preview in the Metro/a review in the Standard! I see everything I do. You can't keep me away. Shall I read you it? Here, let me read it. It's not as though anything's happening, is it! It's not as though we're going to miss anything!

Here.

ADRIAN reads from a newspaper – a review or a preview of this play.

Yes, blah. Yes, well! Doesn't say anything really! Does it?

Space.

Everyone's looking at me! My face isn't ready for this level of attention! Don't look at me! Don't!

I've only just had the stitches out!! The bandages off! Look! Almost good as new!

Space.

Oh, we're all so gorgeous, aren't we? Look at us. Look!

I think we're better looking than the actors, don't you? Do you, _____? Do you? Look at us. Look. We're gorgeous.

Maybe not better looking... But more realistic!
More chance of a snog from one of us than from
the Prince of Denmark, don't you think! Do you,
_____?

And you *are* looking at the kind of man who
likes to hang around the stage doors! Don't you,
_____? I waited for ages for Ralph Fiennes
once after some French play. An incurable
romantic, I am. I can't help it! Aren't you?
_____? No? All that glamour? I can't resist it!

Making up for a thoroughly normal life. Do you
have a normal life, _____? Do you? What do
you do? That's fantastic! Isn't that fantastic? Not
normal at all? Is it? What about you? What do
you do? That's fantastic, too! Isn't it?

I think it is.

Space.

Oh, we're gorgeous.

But I often think – I think – I think that
sometimes the most fantastical – the most made
up thing in the theatre is us! Don't you, _____?
I saw a play last year. And I remember thinking,
'that writer has imagined me'. I've been
imagined! Poorly imagined! The audience has
been badly written.

We're all going to have to *pretend ourselves!* Do
you know that feeling, _____?

Space.

And the actors just go on and on and on, don't
they? About the state of the world or why they
can't get laid. Or they smash each other's brains
in! And we just let them, don't we? That's what
we expect of them, isn't it _____. It's what we

love, isn't it. We wouldn't be here. No one ever asks them to stop, do they? And the lights flash on and off and there's loud music and shouting.

I can't do flashing lights!

And everything's always so promising before the play begins! Before they open their mouths. That's the best moment, _____. We're all so expectant. We're all being so lovely! And then the lights go down.

There's always hope, isn't there, _____. Hope is what brings us back, isn't it? Again and again and again. The hopeful moment! Are you hopeful, _____? Where are you with hope, _____?

Without hope, what is there? Do you agree, _____?

Look at us. Look at all our lonely, hopeful hearts!! Sitting here. Staring out! Hoping for something to happen. Waiting for someone to talk to us. Really talk.

An audience member in the middle of a block gets up and leaves. They are helped to leave by an usher.

You say something then!

The door closing.

You say something.

A beat.

Music plays.

Houselights go out, one by one, slowly, visibly. The audience becomes beautifully lit, slowly, visibly. Their light contained on them, with darkness all around.

Music stops.

Space.

TIM: I'm led downstairs by a young woman with
         her hair pulled back and held in place with a
         large plastic tortoiseshell hair grip – like sharp
         teeth chomping down on the back of her head!
         Ha! She's wearing a dress that makes her look
         a little like a nurse. She looks really clean. Like
         she'd smell really clean. I think about her being
         naked. Even at this time, in this state, I think
         about her naked and stretched out for me! Can
         you imagine? I look at the shape of her breasts. I
         think about the weight of her breasts.

         She asks if I have ever used a floatation tank
         before and I say no. I say that this was a gift.
         I was given a token as a gift. A voucher. From
         the theatre, I tell her, as if she might be even
         remotely interested. The sound designer gave
         us tokens on the last night of a play I wrote,
         I say! I'm Tim Crouch, I tell her, the author.
         She looks blank. She hasn't heard of me! The
         sound designer of the play, I say, my play, said
         we looked like we all needed some sensory
         deprivation! It's taken me three months to
         redeem it!

         I've been looking forward to it, I say. Ha ha. I
         talk too much when I'm nervous!

         My mouth is dry.

Space.

         She shows me the tank. It's sitting in the middle
         of the room like an oversized sarcophagus.
         She opens it up – lifting two flaps at the near
         end, like trapdoor hatches that come to rest on
         their hinges facing up to the ceiling. Her dress
         is pressed across the curves of her young body.
         I imagine her legs opening for me, her dress

lifting up. Her soft flesh opening up for me. I imagine I –

Space.

Is this okay?

Is it okay if I carry on?

Do you want me to stop?

Do you?

Do you?

Space.

The tank is moulded fibreglass – and the water is maybe only a foot deep. She shows me the light switch and the alarm button. She says the water is at blood temperature. Ha ha! At blood temperature! She says she hopes I have a good time. I thank her and she leaves me.

Space.

I'm sorry.

Someone else go.

Space.

VIC: Tim said, with a monologue, the most important thing is to know who you're speaking it to. To whom you're speaking it. Do you understand?

You can't just say, oh, I'm speaking it to myself. Or, I'm thinking out loud. Or, I'm just talking to 'an audience' in 'a theatre'! You can't just pick a spot above the audience's head and deliver it into the middle distance! You have to give the audience a character, a relationship to you. Doesn't matter if you can't see them. Something has to be at stake for the audience. They have to maybe need convincing of something, or

persuading of something or rousing or enlisting.
Imagine them as a child or – or a confessor.
Enlisting is a good one! I'm enlisting you! Or
they need seducing or pleasuring. Pleasing,
I mean. But do you understand? Then the
relationship between me and the audience is
alive, is real, not rhetorical but active. Something
is at stake. Tim said you should get them to a
point where they almost feel able to answer
back. Or shout out.

So, I'm, let's say, 'provoking' you! Or maybe
'rousing', or 'stirring' or something!

What do you think?

Really.

What do you think?

Can you see all right?

Space.

TIM: There's music playing ever so quietly in the
room. I take my clothes off, fold them, hang
them up. It says on the voucher I'm supposed to
wear trunks but I haven't brought any. I didn't
bring any. It doesn't matter anyway. I stand for a
moment in front of a mirror above a sink. I look
at myself, at the offending articles. Ha ha. The
guilty party.

I reach into the pocket of my jacket and take out
a pen and a pad of Post-it stickers. I rest the pad
against the sink and write a note. My hand is
shaking! I peel off the sticker and place it on the
outside of the hatch of the tank.

I mount the two steps that take me over the
threshold and then step down into the water. It
feels warmer than blood, but then when have I

ever stepped into a pool of blood? Really, ha ha
ha? I am holding a small plastic box in my hand.

Inside the box is a sharp blade, a cutting blade,
like a scalpel. The sharpest thing I could find in
the house! In Jules's studio. In my wife's studio.

I hold on to the grips on either side and lower
myself down. I reach up for the handles of the
trapdoor hatches and bring them together,
closed above my head. Like this.

(The author re-presents the action.)

Can you see?

I lie back in the warm salt solution and my
body bobs up like a cork! It's wonderful! The
light inside the tank is still on. I float there in
suspension. The music they have been playing
has faded out. I am gripped with panic, ha
ha. I don't yet feel able to switch out the light.
Not that there's anything to see. I tip my head
forward and look down at my toes and then
back up to the roof of my coffin!

Space.

VIC: I played the part of Pavol in the play. The father.
The abuser in the title. Tim said at the audition
that life has not been good to Pavol, and that
Pavol has not been good to life! That's brilliant, I
said, and laughed and hated myself for sounding
like a middle class idiot, rather than the monster
I hoped they'd employ me for.

I still think they made a mistake in the casting.
I wouldn't hurt a fly, let alone rape one with a
broken bottle!

I mean, look at me.

Listen to me.

Space.

TIM: Here I am, I think. The prize-winning
playwright. Entombed in the basement of a
building. On the outskirts of a city. On the day
that there are tanks at the airport. There are
soldiers being flown home in coffins. There
are photographers outside my house. The
celebrated author. His location unknown to his
wife and children and to the world! The famous
playwright. Darling of the universities.

The lights very slowly fade out.

Near darkness. Silence.

In the dim light.

ESTHER: Has anyone here ever marched against the war?

Anyone?

I remember the day the theatre marched against
the war! Would you like me to tell you? Yes?

Would you?

Would you?

It was a West End or an Equity thing organised
to go along with a public demonstration.
An anniversary of the war starting. We were
encouraged to go in bits of costume or make-
up. Can you imagine! The cast of Mamma
Mia, Lord of the Rings, Spamalot, Les Mis,
Hairspray, The History Boys, Wicked, Stomp,
Joseph, The Lion King! All those actors! Actors
from all those shows – singing their songs and
dancing. The Billy Elliot cast dancing! I was in
High School Musical at that time – fresh from
Drama Centre. I was only 21. We took our pom
poms! Not everyone went, of course. Some
people were opposed to it. And there were

companies from the National and the non West End theatres – the Tricycle, the Bush, the Royal Court, the serious ones who looked down their noses at us! But we didn't care, anyway. Not then, on the march. We were having fun!

And look at me now – at the Royal Court Theatre!

Those of us who hadn't made their own banners were able to pick up ready-made ones from various posts along the route. The most popular was one with a picture of a dead girl from a recent bombing and the slogan, 'Not One More Death'. Do you remember that image? It was an amazing day. We sang 'We all live in a terrorist regime', to the tune of Yellow Submarine! In my High School skirt and pig tails! All those trained voices! No wonder we were on TV!

Of course everyone had to get away for the matinees.

There were banner collection points but people had just dropped them outside the underground. We weren't allowed to take them on public transport. There were piles of the banners and we had to walk over them to get to the underground. It was weird walking over the photograph of the dead girl. Her dead eyes staring up at us. I had real difficulties in the matinee, wanting to cry. About the war and the dead girl.

Space.

Would you like me to sing for you?

Would you?

Yes?

Would you?

When an audience member says 'Yes', she sings some of a song from a West End musical.

The lights fade up very slowly over her song.

Space.

VIC: Do I look like a monster?

            Do I?

            I mean I mostly play sports teachers! Or corrupt
            policeman. Or whatever they give me, I'm not
            complaining. I went through a period of playing
            gays. I played a psychotic gay on The Bill! My
            girlfriend got quite worried about me – kissing
            all those blokes! Maybe it's the hair that does
            it – makes people think I'm queer or hard or
            something. Or both! I can't do anything else
            with it.

ESTHER: I played the part of Eshna in Tim's play. The
            daughter. The abused.

VIC: I should get a wig.

Space.

TIM: I switch the light out.

Space.

ESTHER: It was the hardest role of my career.

TIM: And I'm crying. Like a baby. Ha ha! Poor taste!
            Howling like a baby!

ESTHER: My husband knows how I feel about theatre. He
            said there was no question I should do it. Don't
            think about the money, he said.

TIM: I think I want the young woman to hear me. Someone to hear me. To come and hold me and stop me. To climb inside here with me.

ESTHER: I love the live-ness of theatre. The relationship with the audience. I do too much telly.

TIM: My own warm salty water joining the warm salty water around me.

ESTHER: I don't do enough theatre.

TIM: I cry and cry and cry.

ESTHER: You've probably all seen me in a certain low-budget film about some teenagers.

               Yes?

TIM: I shiver in the warm.

ESTHER: Or on the television.

TIM: I want to press the button.

ESTHER: Or in the papers.

TIM: I want to stop this.

ESTHER: It was the hardest thing.

Music.

Space.

TIM: The play was a poem, really. A personal lament. The violence is there as an underscoring to the central relationship. The father and his daughter. The abuser and the abused. A way of getting the characters closer to each other, just a dramaturgical device, really. The violence is not the most important thing, which some of the reviewers seemed to suggest. But it can't be avoided. I mean look around us.

Society is defined by its edges, isn't it? Not by its centre.

I think I'd become more and more absorbed by images from the edges. I think we all had! Just through everyday exposure, really. And a hunger to see what was going on. What had become possible in the world we lived in.

What had become recently possible.

Or possible again.

Riven flesh, severed limbs, decapitated heads.

Is that okay? Decapitated heads, ha ha.

Space.

ADRIAN: I always book my tickets right when the season is announced. You know. I booked for this ages ago. Did you? When did you? Do you get a concession? Do you mind me asking? How much did you pay? Do you mind saying? _____? Online? What about you, _____? Do you live near here?

TIM: I never felt it was surprising. It became a small hobby of mine – like stamp collecting, ha. Not a collector, but an assembling, an assemblager – placing image against image. I took it upon myself to look at images of abuse, at beheadings, for example! To follow all the links on my computer.

To download and transfer and assemble.

To explore how these pictures fashion our relation to one another. To assemble and reassemble. On stage, I suppose. To bombard myself with all the gory details! It was remarkably easy to find. Harder almost not to. My gorgeous wife asked how I could look at images like these, let alone in a theatre. How can we not? I replied. If we do not represent them then we are in danger of denying their existence.

She deals with all this by cooking fabulous meals and spoiling the children! That's her way of dealing with it.

The unbearable image.

Is that a fair way of putting it?

Space.

My god, when I think about it, we're incredibly lucky.

My god, we're blessed!

Space.

ADRIAN: I'm a 'Friend'! A Friend of the Royal Court Theatre! That's why I see everything. I might know nothing about it. I just agree to see everything. I book at the beginning of the season. I trust them. The people who run the theatre. I'm rarely disappointed. And...I get a discount! Yay! You get £5 off the top ticket prices and you get a newsletter, an email. And you can book tickets earlier than anyone else. Is anyone else a 'Friend'? Anyone here? _____? _____? Are you? Well done us! Hooray! We're friends! We're helping to secure the future of new writing.

Sorry. Sorry. I'll stop. You go. You go on.

Space.

ESTHER: The first question everyone would ask is, 'What's the blood made out of?'

TIM: My intention was to deliver a shock – to create a – an amateur war zone on the stage – like a

178

physical blow. A simulation of a physical blow. To represent what was happening in the real world. To show what was happening. Not in my life, of course, thank god, I'm incredibly lucky. But what I perceived. What we all perceived. The ethics of the images we saw. To push that to the extreme.

Art operates in the extreme.

And, of course, I was angry because we were at war. But it didn't have to be the war.

Space.

ESTHER: 'What's the blood made out of!'

ADRIAN: You should become Friends! Become a subscriber. Seriously. Everything they do here is good. Is great! It has an international reputation! I have a friend who lives in New York but he sees everything here. We don't know how lucky we are to have this on our doorstep. British theatre is the best in the world.

TIM: You know how a stubbed toe can sometimes release the flood-gates! The unexpectedness of physical injury – a slap or a knock. You didn't know you felt that way, but then a knock or a slap, er, reveals how you feel.

Music.

Space.

ADRIAN: The title of the play referred to the girl in it, I suppose. It was her face on the poster, in the brochure – looking dreadful. Although it was more about the father and the war or whatever. I knew her because I'd seen her before – in that film where she was the girl. I didn't know him, though, the father. I thought he was marvellous.

And of course I knew of the writer – who was also directing.

TIM: Or even missing the bottom step can invoke a feeling of incensed outrage at the invasion of the physical – into our ordered little world! Our protected little lives. You know?

ADRIAN: I'd wanted to see the first night, the press night. I love the press nights and as a Friend it's sometimes possible to get tickets because mostly, for the press night, they just go to the press and invited, you know, guests! Not plebs like us! But I was ill that time and they offered me another date. I was still ill, but I was determined to see it before the run ended, so I went on the last night. I shouldn't have gone. I knew there were flashing lights. It said it in the theatre. On signs in the theatre. Flashing lights and nudity. I'm a delicate flower! I blame it on myself.

ESTHER: 'What's the blood made out of!'

ADRIAN: I'm a lot better now. Don't you think? Look! I can see now. All better! There was a moment when they thought I'd lose an eye. A detached retina! A fractured socket. Sounds gruesome, doesn't it! But I'm really fine now. I really am! Don't you think, _____?

TIM: Here I am, a civilised man, a theatregoer. A writer.

ADRIAN: I missed the last fifteen minutes, didn't I? But I thought it was amazing anyway. So powerful. Really intense. Too intense. In such a small space and no air and all that gory stuff. And there was air conditioning! It was amazing! The critics couldn't make up their mind, but I wouldn't have missed it. I loved it.

The actors were so brave!

Did anyone else see it?

A sudden black out.

Space.

Lights up.

VIC:	I thought they'd give it to someone foreign, Pavol. A real foreign actor. I'm Welsh, but...
	At the audition, we read from the play and Tim asked if I was okay about being in something like that, having to do the things my character has to do – you know, the sex and violence. He said:
TIM:	Your agent said she thought you'd be okay.
VIC:	I'm an actor!
	I didn't tell them that I hadn't worked for a year!
	Before rehearsals began we did some work on the accents and I spent a week with Tim – just exploring the character of Pavol. Didn't we?
TIM:	Yes.

Space.

ESTHER:	I played the part of Eshna in Tim's play.

Space.

TIM:	In rehearsal we all watched a mobile phone film of some soldiers taking it in turns to rape a prisoner. To make her pregnant. It was posted on a website. Can you imagine? That I can tell you that we watched that? That I'm here, telling you that! Can you believe that?
	I rewrote quite a bit after that!
ESTHER:	I played the part of the daughter.

TIM: Am I right? Look around you and tell me that
            this world is not full of horrors. Look around
            you.

            Look.

            Look.

            Can you see all right?

Space.

ESTHER: I couldn't do any of the early preparation before
            rehearsals because I was having a baby! Or
            rather, I had had a baby and I wanted to be with
            him as long as possible before I went back to
            work.

ADRIAN: What's his name?

ESTHER: His name's Finn. He's eight months now. I have
            a photograph of him. Would you like to see him?

            Would you?

            Yes?

            Would you?

She shows a couple of photographs – passes them around.

            He's beautiful, isn't he?

            I'd worked with Tim before, hadn't I?

TIM: Yes.

ESTHER: I did a play of his at Soho. We'd got on really
            well – quite intense, really. I was going through
            a really hard time and he was great. A couple
            of years ago. Before my film came out. Before
            I married Paul. I'd got to know his family. I'm
            friendly with his family, his wife, Jules. Tim
            really wanted me for the part. He even named
            the character after me! And he was great about

my situation, the baby. My concern was that I wasn't young enough for the part. She's meant to be sixteen.

Space.

VIC: We spent a lot of time on the computer – watching reports, understanding the situation. Looking at images. Some people said that the things that happened in the play were too extreme, but they're nothing to what we looked at.

We even took a cheap flight and actually spent a couple of days over there. It's still a dangerous place. Tim wrote about the trip for the *Guardian* and was taking photographs for his blog.

We kept on saying, 'There's a Pavol!' and 'There's Pavol!' It was amazing. Life is totally brutal there. The effects of the war. Young men with deformities pushing themselves around on skateboards. Without their shirts, so you see the open wounds or the twisted spines. Like Cardiff on a Friday night!

Tim talked about the play – about violence in a culture, about what happens to you when you live with that violence around you all the time. About how we have to recognise it, confront it, absorb it. We have to show it. He talked about how the human body is distorted, no – what was your word?

TIM: Abstracted.

VIC: Abstracted. Abstracted by the violence. I don't know. To be honest, I must say that I never really understood. But it's not my job to understand. I didn't write it. It's not the kind of play I'd go and see.

ESTHER: I've always looked younger than I am. But
           having a baby. Tim said that he wouldn't feel
           happy about a real young girl doing it – being
           exposed to those things. He said that the public
           would not be comfortable about that. That he
           would get the theatre into trouble.

VIC: We looked at the people. Tim talked about
           how the violence of the culture is shown in the
           bodies of the people we saw – the way they
           sit – like this. Or the way they hold their anger
           and despair. I understood this. As an actor, I
           understood this. I work through the physical.
           From the outside in.

           In here, in the shoulders like this. Moving like
           this. Their arms like this.

He performs an action with his shoulders. ESTHER joins in.

           Do you want to try that?

           Everything we did was to help to tell the story.

ESTHER: Is everyone okay? Can you all see okay?

VIC: We went out one night, away from the hotel.
           With a guide who carried a gun! We talked to
           some men. In the back room of an underground
           bar that our guide had organised. I really found
           Pavol there, I suppose. One man, whose family
           had been killed in one of the massacres. Whose
           son had been stood against a wall with other
           men from the village and shot. By the militia or
           someone. He showed me an old photograph of
           his son. And I brought that man back with me
           to London! In my overhead luggage, Tim said!
           Took him into the rehearsal room. Shared him
           with the production team.

           It was the most useful thing.

Lights fade out.

Space.

Lights up.

ESTHER: On the first day of rehearsals Tim gave us jobs
           to do. Didn't you?

           We had to go out into the city and find someone
           who connected with the themes of the play. We
           had to study them and interview them and then
           bring back what we'd observed. It was brilliant
           because we'd done loads of that kind of stuff at
           Drama Centre. I went to a shelter for women
           who had suffered domestic violence. I was really
           lucky. I met a woman who had been raped as
           a teenager by her father. That's just like my
           character, I said!

Space.

VIC: But it's the quality of the writing, you know?
           It's not me, it's the writing. You know it's well
           written when it gets inside you. It really got
           inside me. There's only so much research you
           can do as an actor, but if it's not backed up by
           the writing.

           You know?

Space.

ESTHER: Her name was Karen. She was like this. Can you
           see that? Her tension here. Her eyes like this. A
           filthy track suit.

Space.

TIM: Hello Karen.

ESTHER: Yeah.

TIM: Thanks for agreeing to talk with us.

185

ESTHER: I'm not –

TIM: It's okay. We're just really pleased that you could be here with us. Aren't we? We just wanted to get to know you, really, to hear a little bit about you. We're really interested in you, aren't we? Aren't we?

VIC: Yes!

ESTHER: Yeah?

TIM: Do you want to talk about what happened to you? About why you're here?

ESTHER: What?

TIM: In this place.

ESTHER: In the shel'er?

TIM: In the shelter or in the theatre. It's up to you. Wherever you want to be.

ESTHER: I don't wanna be 'ere.

TIM: That's fine! We're not here! We can be wherever you want!

ESTHER: Don't fuckin' wanna be 'ere.

VIC: That's fine.

TIM: Do you want to talk about your dad?

ESTHER: No.

TIM: We understand. It won't go any further than this. Do you want to tell us about what he did? What he made you do?

ESTHER: No.

Stuff.

TIM: What kind of stuff?

ESTHER: Stuff.

TIM: Did he hurt you?

ESTHER: I ain't a fucking kid.

VIC: It's all right, Karen.

ESTHER: I ain't a fucking kid.

TIM: Of course.

ESTHER: Films and pictures and stuff.

TIM: What?

ESTHER: What do you fuckin' think?

TIM: I know how difficult this must be for you.

Space.

            Do you want to carry on?

ESTHER: I never –

TIM: And what did he do?

ESTHER: He put things – filmed me with his mates.
            Putting things inside me. What you fucking think
            he did? Read me fucking story books?

TIM: I'm so sorry.

ESTHER: No you're not. You're not fucking sorry. None of
            you are fucking sorry.

VIC: How old were you when it started, Karen?

ESTHER: –

TIM: How old, Karen?

ESTHER: Twelve.

VIC: Twelve.

TIM: How did that make you feel, your dad doing those things?

          Karen?

ESTHER: Can we stop, Tim?

Space.

TIM: Would anyone else like to ask Karen any questions?

          You're happy to improvise, aren't you, Esther?

ESTHER: –

TIM: Are you okay about that, Karen? If other people ask you some questions?

ESTHER: –

TIM: Anyone? Would anyone else like to ask Karen any questions?

          Anyone?

Maybe some questions are asked of Karen by members of the audience.

ADRIAN: I'd like to ask a question.

TIM: Of course.

ADRIAN: What was it like working with Daniel Craig?

ESTHER: I never had any scenes with him, really.

TIM: This is Karen we're asking, not Esther.

          I think we should thank Karen for coming in and Esther for bringing her.

They clap 'Karen'.

Space.

More Space.

VIC: We worked on the world of the play and the
             relationships. It was harrowing sometimes –
             pushing ourselves deeper and deeper into the
             truth of it. The relationship between Pavol and
             his daughter. The manipulation and abuse.
             Improvising and improvising. And then working
             on the text. Working to establish the contact
             between the characters – the psychological
             action. Finding the truth of the story in each
             moment.

ESTHER: I'm not saying that my character was Karen.
             It wasn't an impersonation. I think that if she
             had come to see the play she wouldn't have
             recognised herself. It was just incredibly helpful
             to have her as – as a reference point.

VIC: The guy we met over there. I was hot-seated
             as him, in the rehearsal room here! Just here,
             by the side of the building. I had to physically
             bring him in, in me. I smashed a table, do
             you remember? That poor stage manager,
             Nicky, was in tears! She spent ages finding that
             rehearsal table! And I wanted to apologise to her
             and Tim said, don't apologise, Pavol wouldn't
             apologise. Do you remember?

TIM: Yes!

VIC: Tim was amazing – he would push me to
             places I didn't know were inside me. Esther,
             who played Eshna my daughter, was terrified
             sometimes. Weren't you?

ESTHER: Yes!

VIC: I perfected this dead look behind the eyes. It was
             mentioned in the reviews. Like this! I can't do
             it now, but it used to really upset my girlfriend.
             See? This? See? She almost called the police
             once. She almost called the police! Something

she felt had gone too far one time. She said I had
gone too far. But I couldn't leave Pavol in the
rehearsal room. I couldn't leave him on stage.
I really tried! He would come home with me.
'Leave me alone!'

Space.

ESTHER: But I think that's why the play was so successful.
            Or so powerful. The audience could see that
            we'd done our research, you understand, they
            believed us. The fear looked so real. They left
            the theatre absolutely stunned. In shock! Tim
            would come in every now and then during
            the run, wouldn't you, and was unbelievably
            encouraging. He would illuminate depths to the
            meanings.

Space.

VIC: She said it had changed me. That I wasn't the
            man that she knew.

TIM: You write and write and discover and discover.
            And then you let go. You hand over. You leave
            it to the actors. They will make their own
            discoveries. You leave it to your audience.

VIC: I had lost my joy.

TIM: There were a lot of ideas in my head. A lot
            of images. My job was to find a story that
            would contain those ideas, those questions. A
            relationship. That's the job of a writer. Not to go
            in and solve things. But to reveal things, things
            for other people to solve. To present the truth of
            the story.

VIC: I wasn't fun any more.

Space.

ESTHER: Oh, yes! We spent a lot of time with a special effects guy from a film studio. And Malcolm the fight director.

TIM: It wasn't my story.

ESTHER: Malcolm was amazing.

TIM: Some people thought, I suppose, that maybe I had experienced things like that – in my childhood. But nothing could be further from my truth! Ask Jules. I had researched them, but my job is to represent them, not to have lived them.

ESTHER: I had pouches of stage blood strapped to bits of my body. One famous moment when Vic would hit me in the face and blood would spray from my eye. I had a sponge in my hand, so when I brought my hand up like this – like this, can you see? – I could make the blood spray out. Nobody knew how it was done! It was really shocking and real. The stage was a mess at the end of the show. Poor old stage management spent hours clearing it up at the end. I had to shower for ages to get it all off me!

TIM: Confronted by the death of his wife. Confronted by his daughter in the ruins of his home. His daughter who demands from him a new start, a fresh perspective. A salvation. The younger generation demanding change from the older. Something which cannot be accomplished. Which is why he starts to abuse her, brutalise her, mutilate her.

ESTHER: And a bag strapped to my inner thigh – here – with raw liver in it. So when Vic reached his hand up inside me and tears away at my womb – he just reached into that bag. My god, people would gasp at that moment, groan, faint!

TIM: The play was a psychological study. It's not
             meant to be taken literally. It's an allegory.

Space.

A brilliant light-show plays across the audience.

Space.

ADRIAN: Would anyone like a Malteser? _____? I haven't
             got enough for everyone.

*ADRIAN hands out a few Maltesers to the people whose names he has
come to know.*

             This is the safest place in the world! Don't you
             think, _____? Safe, in here? Where are you with
             safety? I mean, nothing really happens in here,
             does it? Not really. Nothing real.

             I get here and I go flop! I go, phew! It feels
             like in here anything is possible and it's safe.
             It's all safe! I've seen everything imaginable
             here. I've seen bum sex and rimming and cock
             sucking and wankings and rapings and stabbings
             and shootings and bombings. Bombings and
             bummings!! I've seen someone shit on a table!
             I've seen a man have his eyes sucked out. I've
             seen so many blindings! And stonings. Um. I've
             seen a dead baby in a bag. A baby stoned to
             death. I've seen a dead baby get eaten! That was
             great!

             It's such an education! Isn't it? Isn't it, _____?

             And nobody knows! Nobody knows! The cars
             and buses go round and round outside and
             none of them have any idea. No idea at all. That
             we're here, in here, safe in here, enjoying our
             Maltesers and our bum sex. It's a private club
             for the depraved!! Don't you think, _____?
             There's no danger of it going any further

because we're all consenting adults. All of us, all us dirty mother-fucking cunts!!

I'm sorry. That's a horrible thing to say! Sorry. Sorry. Sorry. I'm sorry. I'm sorry. Sorry.

Quite free-ing, though!

And it doesn't matter. It doesn't matter anyway because nobody out there knows and nobody out there really cares. Do they?

Oh, I love this.

So on the last night of the run I saw the play. Well, saw *most* of the play! Who was it who said that – some critic – 'sodomy and vomit'!

TIM: The press were pretty good, really. They had nothing but praise for the two actors. Some failed to get the poetics, really. They all commented on the visceral, er, experiential quality of the writing. And, of course, the more gruesome aspects of the production. On the whole, though, positive. We were sold out almost before we opened. A lot of them had come to see Esther, I think. There had been an article about her in a Sunday newspaper.

Space.

ESTHER: He's an American contractor. An engineer, Tim said. The man is kneeling up, slightly to the right as we're looking at it – left of the camera. I suppose if you looked for it you would say he looks tired. But you don't think about things like this when you see him because your heart is in your mouth. You only notice these things after you've watched it a number of times.

We saw maybe 15 different ones. Over and over. We had to go away and find them. And we'd

recreate them in rehearsal. For the end of the
play.

TIM: I would pop in and out of the run – to see how
they were coping. Sit and watch. Meet up with
Vic and Esther afterwards, give a few notes.
Hearing stories of audience responses – standing
ovations, faintings! I think our work in rehearsal
really paid off.

ESTHER: One where the hostage is just shot unexpectedly
and everyone in the frame jumps out of their
skin. It's almost funny. Maybe the gun went off
by mistake, but the man's head is blown apart.

One with a sword like they do in Saudi Arabia
– with the man crying and crying and begging
for his life – an Italian – and two men having
to almost lie down on the floor on either side to
hold him upright.

This image of the engineer is held for some
time – just the sound of the birds and the child
occasionally – or maybe not a child. I don't
know. I don't know. It could be a television on
somewhere. There's a sense of expectation. It
doesn't feel like a place where this will happen,
you know. The American contractor doesn't
know where to look. At one point he looks at the
camera. Maybe he doesn't know it's on. Maybe
he doesn't know what's going to happen.

Are you all okay?

Are you okay if I carry on?

Space.

ADRIAN: I sometimes wonder what it would be like to
be an actor in one of those things – you know.
Don't you? I mean they're not really having
their bum fucked or their cock sucked, are

they? Are they? We know that! And there are two hundred people watching them whist they pretend that they are. I wonder if they ever get a bit – you know? I wonder what goes through their mind? So how does that feel? What does that do for their self-esteem, _____? Do you know what I mean? How do they feel when they wake up in the morning?

'Have a good day at work, darling! Be careful when you eat that baby!' And getting paid for it. What's that like, I wonder. Do they have any say in it?

Space.

ESTHER: And then the third terrorist or soldier goes behind the American contractor and he holds the American contractor's head back and the American contractor lets out a gasp and the terrorist is screaming at the camera and he hacks the knife into the man's throat.

VIC: I should have talked to someone during the run.

ESTHER: This one more than any of the others.

VIC: I really went to pieces during the run.

ESTHER: I don't know why.

VIC: I remember taking my girlfriend to a restaurant after one performance – you know, just down here on the King's Road, where they come and cook at your table. And the chef, the Japanese chef, accidentally splashed me with hot oil and I just flipped and pushed him to the ground. There was no release at the end of the play. It just balled up and up. Tighter and tighter.

Space.

ESTHER: I wanted to throw up, go outside. But we had to
            watch it. Nothing else existed in the room apart
            from that thing. Do you understand?

VIC: My girlfriend said that the theatre should pay for
            us both to have counselling – to deal with post
            traumatic stress! I told her don't be daft! It was
            my problem, my thing. It was only a play!

ESTHER: And it happened there, in a room in Chelsea.
            That beheading. With us all gathered around
            the laptop. On a coffee break while we were
            working on Act Two. That's where it happened.
            What were we doing? There. In Chelsea. Here.
            Just here. Just to the side of this building. Just
            past stage door.

Space.

VIC: At the end of each performance we would
            leave the theatre from the stage door and there
            would always be people there. And on the last
            night, Tim had come round to the dressing
            room with a bottle. We all drank quickly – on
            empty stomachs! And the artistic director of the
            building came to thank us. And there was a card
            for each of us from the sound designer with the
            vouchers, and a note from him saying that he
            thought we could all do with a bit of sensory
            deprivation.

ESTHER: I said to Tim, why are we watching this?

VIC: And really I just wanted to leave.

ESTHER: And at that moment music starts to play – Arab
            music. Really loud.

VIC: My girlfriend was very glad when the run
            finished.

ESTHER: And it's terrible. Not the music, but the whole
            thing. And whoever it is is cutting into the
            American's throat. Slicing and hacking. And the
            American is, I suppose, is what you would say
            spasming – jerking. His whole body.

            Like this.

ESTHER performs the actions. She invites the audience to do the same.

            Do you want to do this?

VIC: Tim and I left together. Isn't that right?

TIM: –

VIC: And I left the theatre and there was a crowd,
            mostly waiting for Esther because of the film, but
            also fascinated because of what they'd just seen,
            and it was the last night of the run and there'd
            been so much publicity and so crowding around.
            But not really saying anything – a little shocked
            still I think. No one really recognised Tim, of
            course, but everyone looked at me. I'd been
            terrorising them for the last hour and a half! And
            it's the last night and I'm just wanting to go, to
            get into the underground and go. But there are
            people everywhere. Their faces. Staring at me.
            And it's dark.

ESTHER: And this is a man. Not a goat, or a pig, but a
            man, a man with a wife whom we read about in
            the Observer, with children, a family.

VIC: And then I am approached by someone –
            someone – someone – who comes too close.
            Doesn't he? Would you say, Tim? Tim?

TIM: –

VIC: Too close for that moment, anyway, at the end
            of that show, at the end of the run. With me
            wanting to get away. And his speech is slurred

and his movement is awkward. He seems to trip towards me and is saying something I can't quite make out.

The following three speeches are overlapped.

ADRIAN: I'm so sorry. Sorry I made such a nuisance. I feel terrible. How do you feel? /How does it feel?

VIC: And I put my hand out to keep him away /and he seems to grab hold of it and I think he looks as if he's about to hurt me.

ADRIAN: I thought you were brilliant. You're beautiful. Thank you so much! It's such an amazing play. Sorry I ruined it.

VIC: And then I just lash out.

ESTHER: We put articles on the rehearsal wall. And photographs. Oh God, one photograph of a man whose head had been driven over by a tank. Seriously. Just flat and crushed. It was almost funny. Like stepping on a carton of drink.

VIC: And the crowd take a step or two back. And seem to create an arena. Tim steps back too. And I look at this man who I think is attacking me, and I defend myself. He clings to me and I start to kick him off me. I'm convinced my life is in danger and so I start to kick him. You know? I don't stop to think. Do you understand? It's not hard to understand. Tim? Tim?

ESTHER: I found it difficult to leave the house and get to performances. Not sleeping. Not enjoying my food. Not bearing to have anyone touch me. With Paul or Finn, or at my parent's even. Seeing things. On people's faces. Looking at Finn and his face is black from the bombing. Or when the supermarket delivery comes and I

open the front door, I see the delivery-man with
blood spurting from his throat.

VIC: Is it? He's attacking me. I'm being attacked. And
so I kick and kick – to his legs, then, as he falls,
to his body, then, as he's down, to his head.
I could stop, but I continue. The crowd take
another step back and just watch me. And Esther
is there now, by the stage door.

ESTHER: And questioning what I was doing as a mother.
Bringing a child into a world like this. Finding
it hard to be with him, leaving him with other
people while I took myself off. I suppose a bit of
a breakdown.

VIC: And nobody does anything. And I kick and
kick and kick. And I'm shouting, I suppose. Just
like in the play. And everyone is watching. Just
watching. Nobody tries to stop me. Nobody tells
me not to. So I continue.

ESTHER   I think it's good to cry.

VIC: You cunt. You cunt. Cunt.

ESTHER: It's good to cry. I think it's good.

*The intro of the West End musical song that ESTHER sang earlier starts
to play.*

It means we're getting somewhere. It means
we got somewhere. With the play. There were
nights during the run when I would look out at
the audience on the curtain call and see a sea of
wet faces.

There were nights when Vic and I would clap
the audience. Out of gratitude. Gratitude that
they'd put up with it all. That they hadn't walked
out! I think if it had been us, we would have
walked out. So we would clap them.

ESTHER starts to clap.

The song plays louder and louder.

VIC: Cunt. Cunt.

ESTHER continues to clap.

ADRIAN joins in the clapping.

              Cunt. Cunt.

VIC gets up and leaves the auditorium.

The music ends.

Silence.

TIM: We had a dinner party. Some time after the
              show had finished. Jules had slow cooked lamb
              and pomegranate and she made a Nigel Slater
              lemon meringue ice cream. Our big kids were
              staying with friends. We invited Andy and Karl,
              who directed this. And Vic of course with his
              girlfriend. And Esther and Paul – who had
              brought their baby, Finn. At that age it's easier
              to bring them with you. They sleep so soundly.
              They'd put Finn in a travel cot in the box room,
              my study. It was so lovely to see everyone. Such
              a great group of friends. Such good friends.

The lights start to fade out extremely slowly.

              The meal was a sort of thank you to everyone
              for everything. A recognition that the project
              had been a rather special one. That everyone
              had really put themselves into it.

              Vic had been questioned but the man hadn't
              pressed charges. In fact, he was very apologetic.
              He'd passed out towards the end of the show,
              passed out, fainted, fitted, I don't know. The
              flashing lights. The ushers had taken him
              out without disturbing the play. They'd been

brilliant. He was taken to the bar and been given a cup of tea or something. He was okay. He'd hit his head, bit his tongue or something, which is why Vic was scared or disorientated. The man had blood on his face already when he approached Vic.

Vic was very upset about it. He apologised again to everyone that evening but we all said don't think about it. Don't think about it. No one blamed Vic. We know Vic's not like that.

The lights are nearly out.

We all got drunk. Andy was staying on the sofa in the front room. Karl went back to Richmond. Esther and Paul crashed out in the spare room. They were exhausted with the baby, and Esther had been filming some TV drama thing that day. Vic and his girlfriend left at about 1am. Jules stacked the dishwasher and took herself to bed.

A dim light remaining.

I pour a glass of malt whisky and go to my study. I check my emails and then sit in front of my screen and just meander, really, drift, not really thinking. Not thinking. I type in my password. I am tired but don't feel like going to bed. Images of flesh! I'm not proud, but we've all done it, haven't we? Haven't we? Finn is fast asleep in the travel cot by my side. It's a warm evening. I'm a bit drunk. I feel myself getting big. My throat is dry. I take myself out and just begin to gently fuck myself, you know. We've all done that, at the end of a long day. Haven't we? A couple of clicks.

A couple of clicks before bed!

I see a baby. This baby has a dummy in its mouth.

I have the choice to continue.

I have the choice to stop.

Everyone in the house is asleep apart from me. The baby's skin is damp with sweat from the evening heat, presumably, in this strange house. The image is grainy. The sound of voices from outside, maybe, from the street. A television on somewhere. The room is cramped and untidy. I'm a little shocked with myself.

I turn down the volume.

I decide to continue. Just like that. In a second. Less than a second.

Click. Click.

The baby's dummy is removed and I look at the shadow cast on it. I watch the penis just gently being placed against the baby's mouth and then slowly being pushed in. Not violently, actually. Actually quite gently. Quite lovingly.

I decide to continue.

Everything is muted. My heart is racing. I pull harder. This baby stirs but it does not wake. It does not wake. It has no idea what is going on. It has no idea. When I come, a small amount of cum goes on to the edge of my computer screen. I quickly wipe it off, wipe myself. And join Jules in bed, curling around her lovely warm body and kissing the back of her neck. I am asleep in seconds.

In my meanderings, I forget to log off, forget to shut down, to Delete History.

Of course, when Esther wakes early because her baby is crying. Crying in the box room.

Lights slowly fade up.

ESTHER gets up and leaves the auditorium.

> I thought about taking out my eyes. At first,
> I thought that would be the thing to do. The
> offending articles. Ha ha. The guilty party. But
> this is better. Less classical. Here in the dark. In
> this warm salt solution.
>
> I press the blade into my neck.
>
> Do I continue? The young woman will read the
> Post-It note. She'll know to call the police before
> she does anything else. My wife will not forgive
> me anyway.
>
> You won't forgive me, anyway. I know you.
> Look at you. You won't. You won't forgive me.
>
> Anyway.
>
> Nobody was hurt.
>
> Anyway.
>
> I apologise.
>
> Anyway.
>
> I continue.
>
> The writing is leaving the writer.

The death of the author.

TIM walks out of the theatre.

The houselights are on. The doors to the theatre are open.

The End.

Afterword

To the reader

Well. That was great! How great to be able to read all these plays printed in the order they were written. To have them collected here in one place, to be able to recognise their progress and development, to see and consider their connections.

And now here we are together at the end of the book, you and me. You've made it to the section we've called the *afterword*. The bit where I, Andy Smith (also known as *a smith*, who, alongside Karl James, has worked as a co-director with Tim Crouch on these plays), get to offer you some incisive thoughts about what you've just read.

That's if you've made it through the plays and pages in chronological order, of course. Perhaps you're reading this first. Perhaps you've dipped in and out of the plays; or you've read them in reverse order. Maybe you've only read the one that someone else recommended you read, and now you're idly flicking around wondering what else is here. In any case, whoever you are, whatever you've read and however you arrived at this point, it's good to think of you here. Welcome!

I love these additions to plays, the zones that take us in or bring us out of reading – *after* words and *before* words. I've spent a lot of time considering what to write here, wondering what I can add. Perhaps the introduction whetted your appetite in some way. Perhaps this afterword should be a confirmation of something, a cementing of associations. Perhaps my job here is to bring matters to a close. Conclude matters. Finish things off.

But actually, I'm not interested in that. I don't want to give a sense of finality to anything, especially not here. I want the end of this book to be the beginning of something else. I think (and hope) that now is the time when the thoughts that these plays contain take on some other life – through you and what you do with them. I hope that now you might be thinking about how they relate to you. How you relate to them. You are the reason for these plays' existence. You are the reader and the audience. You are the most important person in the room. And even though I don't know who or where you are, I want you to know that you have been considered – at every step of the way. I am considering you now. I want you to feel invited into and involved in what is going on here. I hope you do.

Maybe it's advice you want. If I have any then, unsurprisingly, it is this: think about your audience. Perhaps you're interested in performing or writing or directing (I recommend being a co-director!). Perhaps you just like reading plays. Whatever your interest, remember your audience. Be them. Rehearse them. Play them. Trust them. Talk about their feelings and their thoughts. Consider and be there for them. You are they and they are you. And you, they – the audience – is where this work happens. And that includes here, in these words that you've just read, at the end of this book that you're holding. And the audience is still working now – after you have put this book down and gone for that walk, made that cup of tea, telephoned that loved one.

Good luck to you.
And thanks.

a smith